QUICK THICK
MACHINE KNITS

QUICK THICK
MACHINE KNITS

MARY DAVIS

Photography by John Melville

A DAVID & CHARLES CRAFT BOOK

ABBREVIATIONS

MY	main yarn
CY	contrast yarn
WY	waste yarn
MT	main tension
UWP	upper working position
LWP	lower working position
NWP	non-working position
HP	holding position
T	tension
Lt	left
Rt	right
st(s)	stitch(es)
carr	carriage
N	needle
RC	row counter
K	knit
dec	decrease
inc	increase
tog	together
1st	first
cont	continue
dc	double crochet (sc in USA)
ch	chain

British Library Cataloguing in Publication Data
Davis, Mary
   Quick thick machine knits. – (A David & Charles craft book).
   1. Machine knitting
   I. Title
   746.432

   ISBN 0-7153-9442-8

Typeset by Typesetters (Birmingham) Ltd
Smethwick, West Midlands
and printed in Singapore
by C S Graphics Pte Ltd
for David & Charles Publishers plc
Brunel House   Newton Abbot   Devon

Distributed in the United States by
Sterling Publishing Co. Inc.
387 Park Avenue South, New York, NY
10016–8810

CONTENTS

INTRODUCTION

Over the past four years of teaching machine knitting it has become apparent that there are very few attractive patterns published for the wide gauge machine. Many of my students, particularly men, have found their initial enthusiasm blighted by the problems of trying to de-code traditional knitting pattern jargon, with which they are not familiar. I hope to have provided something here to dispel the gloom!

A large proportion of the patterns are classic in shape, pattern and style, the sort of garment that I enjoy wearing myself. A basically simple garment becomes special when a beautiful yarn is used. My passion is for colour and I have indulged this to the full in this book.

THE YARNS

There are some beautiful natural yarns available to the home knitter at the moment. If you do not have the time or inclination to dye your own yarn, Colinette's One-Zero is the perfect answer. The vibrancy and intensity of colour are extraordinary. It has been used in combination with mohair in the Lacy Sweater in Mixed Yarns, (p108), and the Full-length Coat (p97), where it complements the rich tones of the mohair.

Colinette's Island wool, used for the Men's Space-dyed Waistcoat (p80), is an aran quality that looks bright and modern. If your taste is for something quieter, there are some wonderful subtle colourways available too.

Mohair of course hardly needs an introduction. A. C. Wood's Mohair Mills have an enormous shade range and no one need feel that he or she has to stick to the colours illustrated. Why not try out your own colour combinations?

On the other hand it takes courage to try knitting in silk. The chunky silk from J. Hyslop Bathgate is however very easy to knit with and produces beautiful results. The pink Mohair and Chunky Silk Jersey (p65) is an example. This uses only a small amount of the silk and so need not be expensive to make. The V-back Cabled Silk Evening Top (p56) is rather more difficult to knit and therefore recommended for the more experienced knitter. The sheen on the silk emphasises the textural patterns formed by the cables.

It is easy to imagine that cotton is the poor relation of silk but this need not be the case. So many people these days complain that they are unable to wear wool. Cotton is very warm and comfortable to wear, and not at all tickly. Most of the double-knitting cotton used here is from A. C. Wood and Texere Yarns. It has a sheen, rather like that of silk, and washes and wears well.

Now to wool. My favourite is the Brora Soft Spun from T. M. Hunter and Jamieson & Smith. It knits so easily and quickly, and the colour range is superb. A close second is the old perennial, Shetland wool, with its companion lambswool. No one should be without these yarns for their versatility and durability. Nethy's shade range is second to none. Many of the garments in the book could easily be adapted to knit in the same way as the Men's All-over Patterned Jersey (p29), with 2 ends Shetland and 1 of lambswool, particularly if like me, you have an enormous stock of Shetland wool.

A recent discovery is the chunky New Zealand cross-bred from J. Hyslop Bathgate. This has a marvellous sheen and feeling of weight as well as a good shade range. Never be afraid to use a 4-ply yarn double as in the Cowl-neck Jersey (p70) where 4-ply lambswool has been used. Designer Yarns supply this, an unusual ply for lambswool which is normally sold in a 2-ply equivalent.

Most of us are used to an aran weight double-knitting and so the Cabled Cricket Jersey (p84) comes as no surprise. Nethy Products supply this yarn but what does come as a surprise is that the girls are wearing this jersey, as well as the boys!

Finally angora – only for the very brave. It is easy to knit with, very warm to wear, but worth its weight in gold. The angora used here from A. C. Wood is 100% angora, the very best, and the style of the Angora Evening Top (p60) absolutely classic as befits a yarn of this quality.

All yarn quantities given in these patterns are approximate and based on very economic use, particularly those supplied by the skein. In the case of Colinette's One-Zero it is advisable to leave very short ends as this yarn does not go far.

THE MACHINES

There is a variety of wide-gauge machines on the market at the moment, including the Bond, the Knitmaster and Brother. All of these machines have the option of à ribbing attachment. The Japanese machines also have an optional charting device, a great asset if you find written patterns difficult to follow. The more sophisticated models have punchcard facilities, Knitmaster a 12-st repeat, Brother a 24-st one. Most machine knitters start off with a standard gauge machine, which normally takes 4-ply yarn, or its equivalent. Not many people realise that thicker yarns may be knitted on these machines using every other needle. Even mohair is a possibility.

The patterns in this book may all be knitted on a chunky machine with punchcard facilities and a ribber. Most can be knitted without a ribber and possibly even without punchcards. The significant factor, as all machine knitters know, is the tension swatch. If you can match the tension you can knit any patttern on any machine, or even by hand!

What follows is a break down of the various patterns and their suitability for different yarns and machines.

PATTERNS SUITABLE FOR CHUNKY MACHINES WITHOUT PUNCHCARDS

Angora Evening Top
V-back Cabled Silk Evening Top *
Sailor-collar Boxy Jersey
Lacy Sweater in Mixed Yarns *
Lace and Fair Isle Jersey *
Raglan-sleeved Cardigan
Cowl-neck Jersey
Tie Design Cardigan
Silk T-shirt
Slash-neck Jersey
Classic raglan-sleeved His and Her Jersey
Men's and Ladies' Cabled Sweater *
Cabled Cricket Jersey *
(Garments marked with a * require hand-tooling)

PATTERNS SUITABLE FOR KNITTING ON STANDARD GAUGE MACHINE USING EVERY OTHER NEEDLE

So long as you are able to match the tension, many of these patterns may also be knitted on the standard gauge machine using every other needle (see below). The tension swatch is knitted over exactly the same number of needles as usual and the same number of rows. It is simply that half the needles are out of work. Once the swatch is complete, pull sharply, lengthwise, to set the stitches. Measure as usual.

If necessary, wax or spray the yarn with silicone, particularly where it is very hairy, or in the case of cotton, lacking in elasticity. This should facilitate the movement of the carriage across the needles.

Angora Evening Top
V-back Cabled Silk Evening Top
Sailor-collar Boxy Jersey
Cowl-neck Jersey
Tie Design Cardigan
Silk T-shirt
Slash-neck Jersey
Classic raglan-sleeved His and Her Jersey
Men's and Ladies' Cabled Sweater
Men's Space-dyed Waistcoat

If you have an electronic machine where the pattern repeat is not limited to 24 stitches, some of the garments with punchcard patterns may also be attempted on the standard gauge. Obviously to transfer a 24-stitch pattern to an alternate needle setting, 48 stitches must be available.

PATTERNS FOR MACHINES WITHOUT A RIBBER

As some yarns, particularly the Brora Soft Spun, make an extra-ordinarily good mock rib, the lack of a ribber need not be a disadvantage. Patterns all adapt well to use of mock rib except those knitted in silk or cotton, in which case a hand-knitted rib would be a better substitute. There are very detailed instructions on how to make mock ribs, both 1:1 and 2:1, on p114. In some cases, for instance, where a garment receives very heavy wear, a mock rib could be a distinct advantage, with double the thickness at cuff and welt. Mock ribs in mohair are also very acceptable as shown on the neckband of the Lacy Sweater in Mixed Yarns (p108). The following patterns do not require ribbing of any kind:

Ladies' waistcoat
Long Floral Jersey
Fleur de Lys Jersey
Men's Space-dyed Waistcoat

PUNCHCARDS

Thoughout this book punchcard on a continuous roll has been used. This has several advantages. Where a pattern extends beyond 60 rows, as for example the leaves on the Full-length Coat (p97), a continuous punchcard eliminates the need to join 2 pieces of punchcard to achieve the length and is therefore neater and simpler. It also avoids wasting odd short lengths of punchcard when a pattern does not require 60 rows.

If you are using 60 row blanks, do remember to check the number of rows with each pattern before punching the card out.

CHARTING DEVICE

Those who have a charting device will be able to follow the diagrams provided with each pattern. There is then no need to match the tension or

even the yarn used. This opens up the way for all sorts of variations on the basic designs illustrated. There is great potential for mixing yarns. I would love to see the Long Floral Jersey (p34) knitted in wool and chenille, or silk, and the borders Swiss-darned with some additional colours.

The Fair Isle jerseys could be knitted in a mixture of wool, cottons and chenille. The Men's Space-dyed Waistcoat (p80) would look very sophisticated in a plain yarn with a very bright-coloured edging. If you use a variety of yarns with a little imagination, beautiful garments will result.

WASHING THE YARN

When preparing to knit any garment in Shetland wool, Brora Soft Spun, lambswool, or chunky New Zealand cross-bred wool, it is important to wash the swatch and dry it before measuring. Most wool brokers provide instructions on how to wash their yarns with their shade cards. You must adhere to these instructions for satisfactory results. Many wools may be steam pressed. Do this before measuring, if the finished garment is going to be treated in this way. There is a marked difference in the measurements of a tension swatch before and after washing.

Jamieson's wools will not need washing in this way, unless they are waxed on the cone, as they are produced for hand-knitters mainly.

WASHING SHETLAND WOOL

1) Wash by hand using lukewarm water and washing soda. Wash strong colours separately, ie scarlet, navy blue, black, royal blue, etc. Always wash white garments separately.
2) Test the water as you would a baby's bath, almost cool. Give the garment two rinses by hand. Do not rub, squeeze gently. If you have an automatic washing machine, put garments into drum for *Cold* rinse and spin, with a fabric softener. If you do not have an automatic

machine, give garment a final cool rinse by hand with fabric softener, then spin dry. Do *not* use a tumble dryer.
3) Hang over clothes airer to dry. *Never* dry on or in front of direct heat, such as a radiator, or fire.

This process applies to tension swatches as well as finished garments. Once dry the swatch may be steam pressed, as may be the garment. It is not appropriate to continue washing Shetland wool garments like this. This process simply removes the industrial oil or wax from the yarn and allows the fibres to expand and soften. Once the oil has been removed the garment may be washed in the normal way for wool.

Any Shetland wool that has been produced for hand knitting eg Jamieson's wool, will not be oiled and consequently will not need this treatment.

TECHNIQUES AND KNOW-HOW

At the back of the book, this section provides basic instruction on the use of a machine together with specific notes on methods employed in the production of the garments illustrated. There are, for example, several ways of making buttonholes and not all will be suitable for all yarns or all garments. It is as well to check with the instructions given and possibly practise on some spare yarn before attempting an unfamiliar method on the final garment itself.

Many yarns lack elasticity; advice is given on the use of knitted-in elastic.

Hand-tooling is also covered. This is considered by some to be old-fashioned, but do please reconsider this view. If you have a chunky machine, the ability to produce lace and cables by manual transfer of stitches is a great asset. The Men's and Ladies' Cabled Sweater (p41) is a beautiful example of this. Manual transfer is a very simple technique that may take a lot of time at first, but once you are accustomed to it, it will become almost automatic.

FAIR·ISLE

Short boxy ethnic-patterned jersey
Men's sleeveless pullover
Fleur de lys jersey with matching hat

Classic jerseys for men and women
Men's all-over patterned jersey

SHORT BOXY ETHNIC-PATTERNED JERSEY

TO FIT

Loose garment with no special fit

Medium: 87–97cm (34–38in)
across chest 53.5cm (21in)
finished length 45cm (17¾in)
sleeve length 45cm (17¾in)

Large: 102–112cm (40–44in)
across chest 57.5cm (22¾in)
finished length 45cm (17¾in)
sleeve length 45cm (17¾in)

YARN

MY – 4×440g hanks black chunky
New Zealand cross-bred wool
1 hank each CY1 – rose, CY2 –
peach and CY3 – raspberry; 2
hanks CY4 – petal
J. Hyslop Bathgate & Co, Victoria
Works, Galashiels, Scotland TD1
1NY

TENSION

T8 throughout
17 sts/22 rows = 10cm (4in)

Please read pattern through
carefully before starting to knit.

BACK

Using ribber cast on 90(98) sts in
MY for 2:1 rib. T0/0, rib 9 rows.
T5/5, rib 1 row. Transfer all sts to
main bed.
RC 000 T8 K 1 row set
punchcard 1. K 1 row start pattern
(33 rows).
RC 38 using short end contrast

yarn place marker at either end
row.
Set punchcard 2, K 1 row and
start pattern.
RC 88 shape back neck as
follows: mark punchcard. All Ns to

Lt centre and 19 to Rt in HP. K 1
row, bring 1 N to HP. K 1 row, etc
until 22 Ns to Rt centre are in HP.
RC 92. Break off both yarns. Set for
stocking st. Thread WY, K 6 rows
and remove from machine.

Card 1
Feeder 1, row 1: CY1
            2   „
            3   MY
            4   „
    rows 5–9   MY/CY2
           10   CY1
           11   „
           12   CY3
           13   „
   rows 14–22   CY3/CY4
           23   CY1
           24   „
           25   MY
           26   „
   rows 27–31   MY/CY2
           32   CY1
           33   „

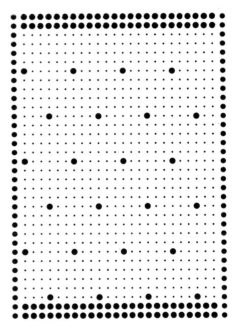

Card 2
Feeder 1, row 1: MY
            2   „
            3   „
            4   „
            5   „ /CY4
    repeat

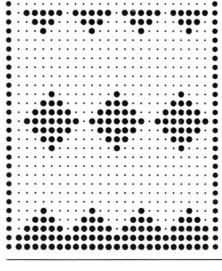

FRONT

As for back to row 72. Carr at Rt, mark punchcard. All Ns to Lt centre in HP and 4 to Rt. K 1 row to Lt, bring 1 N to HP. K 1 row, etc until 22 Ns are in HP. K to row 92. Break yarns. Set for stocking st, thread WY, K 6 rows and remove from machine. Repeat this shaping for Lt shoulder reading Lt for Rt and vice versa. Centre neck sts remain on machine. K 6 rows WY and remove.

FIRST SHOULDER SEAM

With Rt side garment facing, replace sts Lt shoulder on machine. Pull out WY. K 1 row T8 MY. Take 2nd garment piece and replace sts on Ns in work, matching shoulder and with Rt sides tog. K 1 row T8 and cast off.

NECKBAND/COLLAR

Using ribber cast on 98 sts in MY for 2:1 rib. T5/5, rib 30 rows (collar) or 50 rows (roll neck). Transfer all sts to main bed. K 1 row T8. Take main garment piece and with Rt sides tog pick up 1 st on neck edge and place on 1st st rib. This st should be at centre front if collar, or open shoulder if roll neck. Make a loop with a piece of MY and transfer this to the adjacent N. Yarn across N and cast off. Do this for each st. It makes a loose and flexible cast off.

Work second shoulder as first

SLEEVE

Using ribber cast on 40 sts in MY for 2:1 rib. T0/0, rib 9 rows. T5/5, rib 1 row. Transfer all sts to main bed.

RC 000 K 1 row T8 then set punchcard 1. K 1 row start pattern. K as for front and back, inc 1 st at either end of row every 4th row.

RC 86. Break both yarns, thread WY, set for stocking st, K 6 rows and remove from machine.

Turn sleeve round and replace all sts on machine so that Rt side of work is facing you. K 1 row T8 MY. Take main garment pieces, match shoulder seam to centre and markers to edge of sleeve. Pick up sts in between, evenly. K 1 row T8 and cast off. Repeat this for second sleeve.

TO MAKE UP

Back st main seam from cuff to welt. Slip st roll neck edges tog. Slip st cuffs and welts. Weave ends of CY back along line of pattern on reverse side of work.

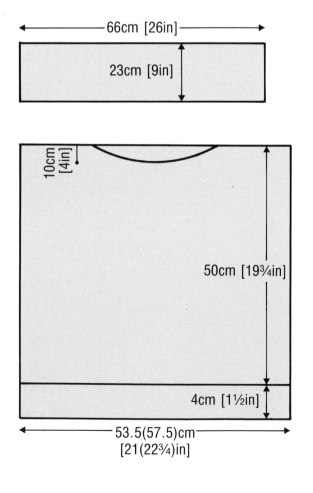

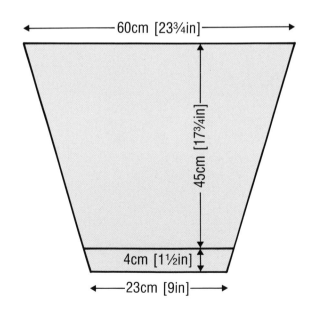

MEN'S SLEEVELESS PULLOVER

TO FIT

Small: 92cm (36in)
across chest 49cm (19¼in)
finished length 59cm (23¼in)

Medium: 97cm (38in)
across chest 51cm (20in)
finished length 62cm (24½in)

Large: 102cm (40in)
across chest 53.5cm (21in)
finished length 65cm (25½in)

Extra-large: 107cm (42in)
across chest 56cm (22in)
finished length 66cm (26in)

5cm (2in) allowance for ease and fit

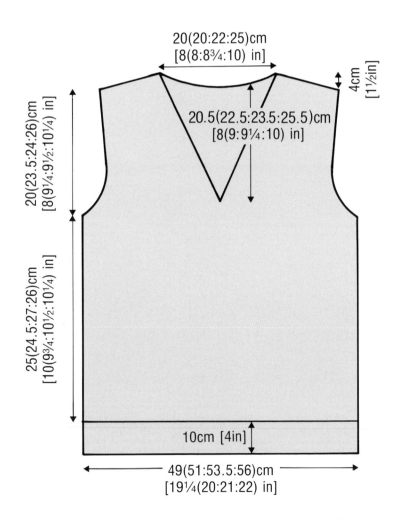

20(20:22:25)cm
[8(8:8¾:10) in]

20.5(22.5:23.5:25.5)cm
[8(9:9¼:10) in]

4cm
[1½in]

20(23.5:24:26)cm
[8(9¼:9½:10¼) in]

25(24.5:27:26)cm
[10(9¾:10½:10¼) in]

10cm [4in]

49(51:53.5:56)cm
[19¼(20:21:22) in]

YARN

MY – 500g Brora Soft Spun BSS39 dark grey fleck
T. M. Hunter Ltd, Sutherland Wool Mills, Brora, Scotland KW9 6NA

Embo 3-ply: CY1 – 3018 blue-green; CY2 – 3019 red; CY5 – 3016 blue (1 × 4oz hank of each)

2-ply Soft Spun: CY3 – BSS11 royal blue; CY4 – BSS10 emerald green (1 × 2oz hank of each)
Jamieson & Smith (Shetland Wool Brokers) Ltd, 90 North Road, Lerwick, Shetland Isles, ZE1 0PQ

These yarns make a very good mock rib. See note on page 114 for instructions on knitting a mock rib.

TENSION

Measured over Fair Isle T8. Swatch washed according to yarn manufacturer's recommendations before measuring
15.5 sts/17 rows = 10cm (4in)

Please read pattern through carefully before starting to knit.

BACK

Using ribber cast on 76(80:84:88) sts in MY for 2:1 rib. T0/0 rib 25 rows, T5/5 rib 1 row. Transfer all sts to main bed. RC 000 carr at Rt. K 1 row T6 then set punchcard. K 1 row, then start Fair Isle. RC 44(42:46:44) carr side cast off 8 sts.

K 1 row, carr side cast off 8 sts. Then dec 1 st at either edge of work every row 4 times and 1 st at either edge of work, every other row 3 times. RC 75(79:85:89) shape shoulders as follows, using HP: at opposite side to carr bring Ns to HP on alternate rows: small 3:2:2; medium 3:3:3; large 4:3:3; extra-large 4:3:3 sts.

RC 78(82:88:92) shape back neck using HP: all Ns to Lt centre and 13(13:14:16) to Rt. Mark punchcard. K 1 row. While cont to shape Rt shoulder bring 1 N to HP on every row, 3 times. 16(16:17:19) Ns to Rt centre in HP.

When all shoulder sts are in HP break MY, thread WY, K 6 rows and remove from machine. Repeat shaping of shoulder and neck edge for Lt side of work, reading Lt for Rt and vice versa. Centre neck sts remain on machine. Thread WY, K 6 rows and remove from machine.

FRONT

Using ribber cast on 76(80:84:88) sts in MY for 2:1 rib. T0/0 rib 25 rows, T5/5 rib 1 row. Transfer all sts to main bed.

RC 000 carr at Rt, K 1 row T6. Set punchcard, K 1 row. Start Fair Isle T8. K in Fair Isle to RC 44(42:46:44). At carr side cast off 8 sts. K 1 row and cast off 8 sts at carr side. K 1 row. Mark punchcard. Shape V neck as follows: all Ns to Lt centre in HP or take back to NWP on nylon cord (see Notes). Working on Rt only, dec 1 st at Rt edge every other row 4 times, then dec 1 st fully fashioned at Lt edge every 2 rows. 10(12:13:13) sts remain. RC 75(79:85:89) carr at Lt, shape shoulder using HP as follows: small 3:2:2; medium 3:3:3; large 4:3:3; extra-large 4:3:3 sts in HP every alt row when carr at Lt.

RC 82(86:92:96) all shoulder sts in HP. Set for stocking st and K 1 row T5. Break MY, thread WY, K 6 rows and remove from machine. Reverse this shaping for Lt shoulder.

FIRST SHOULDER SEAM

Replace sts Lt shoulder back on Ns with Rt side work facing. Pull out WY. With Rt sides tog, place sts Lt shoulder front on same Ns. Pull out WY. K 1 row T6 and cast off.

NECKBAND

Using ribber cast on 71(74:76:84) sts for 2:1 rib in MY. T0/0 rib 9 rows. T5/5 rib 1 row. Transfer all sts to main bed, K 1 row T6. This band goes across the back neck and down one side of the V to the point. The 2nd piece goes from the shoulder seam to the point of the V on the opposite side.

Take main garment piece and with Rt sides tog put all sts on WY at back neck onto Ns in work then pick up evenly along neck edge. K 1 row T6 and cast off loosely, going in front of sinker gates and using a claw weight to stretch the st. *Second neckband piece* Using ribber cast on 39(42:42:46) sts in MY for 2:1 rib. T0/0 rib 9 rows, T5/5 rib 1 row. Transfer all sts to main bed. K 1 row T6 then pick up sts along remaining neck edge as before with Rt sides tog. K 1 row T6 then cast off loosely.

Work second shoulder as first.

ARMHOLE BANDS

Using ribber cast on 78(88:90:96) sts in MY for 2:1 rib. Rib 5 rows T0/0, 1 row T5/5. Transfer all sts to main bed. K 1 row T6. Take main garment piece and with Rt sides tog pick up sts along armhole edge evenly. K 1 row T6 then cast off loosely. Repeat for second armhole.

TO MAKE UP

Slip st welts, ends neckband and armholes. Back st main seam from welt to underarm. Wash garment according to yarn manufacturer's recommendations. Steam press.

Row		
*1	MY	/ CY1
2	MY	/ CY1
3	MY	/ CY2
4	MY	/ –
5	CY3	/ CY4
6	CY3	/ CY4
7	CY5	/ CY1
8	–	/ CY1
9	CY2	/ CY1
10	MY	/ CY1
11	MY	/ CY3
12	MY	/ CY3
13	–	/ CY3
14	CY4	/ CY3
15	CY4	/ CY3
16	MY	/ –
17	MY	/ CY2
18	MY	/ CY1
19	MY	/ CY1
20	MY	/ –
21	MY	/ – *

Fair Isle repeats from * to *, 21 rows in all

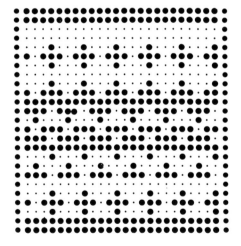

Note: punchcard as illustrated but punch pattern twice so that it will rotate easily in the card reader

FLEUR DE LYS JERSEY
with matching hat

TO FIT

Small: 87–97cm (34–38in)
across chest 60cm (23in)
finished length 68cm (26¾in)
sleeve length 39cm (15½in)

Large: 102–112cm (40–44in)
across chest 68cm (26¾in)
finished length 68cm (26¾in)
sleeve length 39cm (15½in)

YARN

Brora Soft Spun: MY – 1kg BSS36
    dark green; CY1 – 250g BSS12
    purple
    T. M. Hunter Ltd, Sutherland
    Wool Mills, Brora, Scotland
    KW9 6NA
CY2 – 1 hank × BSS21 red
CY3 – 1 hank (2oz) × 3-ply H91
    light pink
CY4 – 1 hank × 2-ply jumper
    weight FC6 dark pink (used
    double)
    Jamieson & Smith (Shetland
    Wool Brokers) Ltd, 90 North
    Road, Lerwick, Shetland Isles,
    ZE1 0PQ

Note: Jamieson & Smith sell their
yarns in very small quantities eg
2oz hanks, for the home knitter

TENSION

Measured over Fair Isle card 1;
swatch is washed first.
T8 18 sts/17 rows = 10cm (4in)

Please read pattern through
carefully before starting to knit.

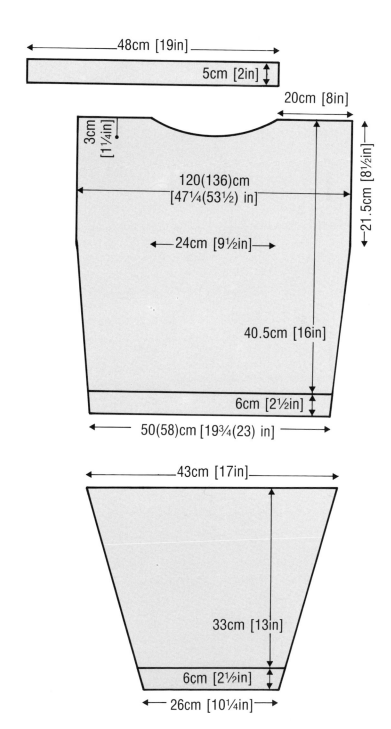

48cm [19in]

5cm [2in]

20cm [8in]

3cm [1¼in]

21.5cm [8½in]

120(136)cm
[47¼(53½) in]

24cm [9½in]

40.5cm [16in]

6cm [2½in]

50(58)cm [19¾(23) in]

43cm [17in]

33cm [13in]

6cm [2½in]

26cm [10¼in]

JERSEY BACK

Cast on 90(104) sts over every other N using WY. K 14 rows MY T3.

Bring all empty Ns into work and K1 row T4, then 1 row T10 and 1 row T4. Start Fair Isle card 2. K 13 rows. Change to stocking st and K 1 row before picking up 1st row of loops.

Set punchcard for Fair Isle card 1. RC 000 K 1 row T8 stocking st Start Fair Isle. Inc 1 st either end of row every 8 rows to 104 (114) sts. RC 66 place marker at either edge of work in contrast yarn. K in Fair Isle to RC 102. Mark punchcard. Carr at Rt, set for Hold. Bring all Ns

to Lt centre and 20 to Rt to HP. K 1 row to Lt, bring 1 more N to HP. K 1 row to Rt, bring 1 N to HP. Cont to bring 1 N to HP each row until 23 Ns to Rt centre are in HP. K to RC 106. Break MY, set for stocking st and thread WY. K 6 rows and remove from machine. Repeat this shaping for Lt shoulder, reversing instructions and reading Lt for Rt. This leaves centre neck sts on machine. Thread WY, K 6 rows and remove from machine.

FRONT

As for back to row 100. Carr at Rt. Mark punchcard. All Ns to Lt centre

Card 1: MY in feeder 1 throughout. Pattern repeats over 5 rows.
Row 1 MY/CY1
    2 „ „
    3 „ „
    4 „ /CY2
    5 „ –

Card 2: MY in feeder 1 throughout. Pattern repeats over 13 rows.
Row 1 MY/CY2
    2 „ „
    3 „ /CY3
    4 „ „
    5 „ /CY4 (used double)
    6 „ „
    7 „ /CY1
    8 „ /CY4
    9 „ „
    10 „ /CY3
    11 „ „
    12 „ /CY2
    13 „ „

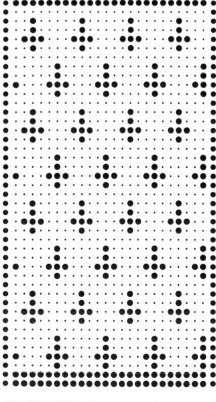

and 18 to Rt in Hold. K 1 row to Lt, bring 1 more N to HP and repeat as for back neck shaping until 23 Ns to Rt centre are in HP. RC 106 break MY, set for stocking st, K 6 rows WY and remove shoulder from machine. Repeat this shaping for Lt shoulder reversing instructions and reading Lt for Rt. This leaves centre neck sts on machine. Thread WY, K 6 rows and remove from machine.

SHOULDER SEAM

Replace sts Lt shoulder, back, on Ns with Rt side garment facing. K 1 row MY T8. Pull out WY. Take front garment and, with Rt sides tog, place sts Lt shoulder on those of Lt back. K 1 row T8 and cast off, going behind sinker gates.

Second shoulder seam is knitted after collar has been attached.

SLEEVE

K 2 alike. Cast on using WY over every other N 48 sts. Make hem as for back. RC 000 K 1 row stocking st MY T8. Start Fair Isle card 1. Inc 1 st either end of 1st row, then every 4th row to 76 sts. RC 54 break MY, thread WY, K 6 rows and remove sleeve from machine. Turn round and replace sts on same Ns. K 1 row MY T8. Pull out WY. Matching shoulder seam to centre pick up along edge main garment pieces evenly between 2 markers, working 1 or 2 sts in from edge. K 1 row T8 and cast off going behind sinker gates.

COLLAR

Cast on using WY 98 sts and K 6 rows. RC 000 set punchcard 2. K 1 row stocking st MY T8. Start

punchcard T3. RC 13 K 1 row T3, 1 row T10, then 14 rows T3 over every other N. (Transfer every alt st to adjacent N after row T10.) Pick up 1st row of loops and replace on Ns. K 1 row T8. Pull out WY. Take back and front garment place sts on WY on those already on Ns. K 1 row T8 and cast off.
Second shoulder seam: replace sts Rt shoulder back on Ns with Rt side garment facing. K 1 row MY T8. Pull out WY. Take front garment and with Rt sides tog place sts Rt shoulder on those Rt back. K 1 row T8 and cast off.

TO FINISH

Back st or mattress st main seam from cuff to welt. On Rt side mattress st hems. Sew in ends of contrast colours. Wash garment according to manufacturer's recommendations, to remove surplus oil and allow sts to close up. Steam press.

HAT

Using WY cast on 102 sts. K 6 rows. RC 000 thread MY and K 1 row T8 before starting Fair Isle card 1. RC 30 start shaping crown using HP and cont in Fair Isle: mark punchcard, carr at Rt, all Ns in HP except 26 nearest carr. Set for Hold. K 1 row. Dec 1 st fully fashioned (double eyelet tool) at either end row every row, 13 times. Pull end of MY through last st.
Bring next 25 Ns to UWP and repeat shaping as above. Repeat for further 25 Ns and finally 26 again.

EAR FLAPS

Using WY cast on 22 sts and K 6 rows. RC 000 thread MY K 1 row

stocking st T8. Insert punchcard 2 and K 1 row. Start Fair Isle T8 and dec 1 st at either end row every other row 9 times. When 13 rows Fair Isle are complete K until 4 sts remain (stocking st). Inc 1 st either end row every other row. RC 36 break MY, K 6 rows WY and remove.

Repeat this for second ear flap.

Counting across 102 Ns used for crown of hat, start at 3rd N in from Rt edge, placing sts on WY at both edges of ear flap, on Ns. Pull out WY. Leave 25 Ns empty before placing sts of 2nd ear flap on Ns and pulling out WY. Take crown of hat and pick up sts on WY placing them on the 102 Ns already in WP. Pull out WY. K 1 row T8 CY2. Insert punchcard 1. K 1 row CY2. Change to MY and start Fair Isle. RC 34 shape crown as before using HP.

TASSELS

Take 3×30cm (12in) lengths MY, 1×30cm (12in) length CY1, 1× 30cm (12in) length CY2 and hold taut. Twist. Fold in half. Knot one end 8cm (3in) from end. Cut this end to form tassel. St opposite end into crown of hat when making up. 2 shorter tassels can be made to hang from ear flaps.

TO MAKE UP

Slip st shaped edges tog. Back st all but 10cm (4in) main seam and pull hat through to Rt side. Mattress st this opening. Slip st edges of ear flaps MY. Push end without stripe CY2 into itself until it meets the opposite end inside. Ear flaps should now hang downwards.

CLASSIC JERSEYS
for men and women

TO FIT

Small (ladies'): 82–87cm (32–34in)
across chest 48.5cm (19in)
finished length 56cm (22in)
sleeve length 43cm (17in)

Medium (ladies'): 92–97cm (36–38in)
across chest 53.5cm (21in)
finished length 64cm (25¼in)
sleeve length 45cm (17¾in)

Medium (men's): 97–102cm (38–40in)
across chest 56cm (22in)
finished length 64cm (25¼in)
sleeve length 56cm (22in)

Large (men's): 107–112cm (42–44in)
across chest 62cm (24½in)
finished length 69cm (27in)
sleeve length 66cm (26in)

Extra-Large (men's): 112–117cm (44–46in)
across chest 63.5cm (25in)
finished length 74cm (29in)
sleeve length 69cm (27¼in)

10cm (4in) allowance for ease. 1cm (0.4in) seam allowance

YARN

MY – 1kg Brora Soft Spun BSS22 navy blue
  T. M. Hunter Ltd, Sutherland Wool Mills, Brora, Scotland
CY1 – 2-ply Soft Spun BSS21 red; CY2 – BSS10 emerald green; CY3 – BSS11 royal blue (2 hanks each)
CY4 – 2 hanks × Embo 3-ply yarn 3018 blue green; CY5 – 1 hank × 3016 dark blue
  Jamieson & Smith (Shetland Wool Brokers) Ltd, 90 North Road, Lerwick, Shetland Isles, ZE1 0PQ

TENSION

Measured over Fair Isle T8. Swatch must be washed according to manufacturer's recommendations
17.5 sts/17 rows = 10cm (4in)

Please read pattern through carefully before starting to knit.

BACK

Using ribber cast on in MY 86(96:100:110:114) sts for 2:1 rib. T0/0 rib 25 rows. T7/7 rib 1 row. Transfer all sts to main bed.
  RC 000 carr at Rt. Set punchcard. T8 K 1 row stocking st. Start pattern and K in Fair Isle. RC 44(52:52:54:62) carr at Rt. Cast off 9(11:11:13:13) sts at carr side. K 1 row. Cast off 9(11:11:13:13) sts at carr side. K. RC 80(92:92:98:106) shape back neck as follows: mark punchcard. Set for Hold. All Ns to Lt centre and 15(15:17:17:18) to Rt in HP. K 1 row to Lt, bring 1 N to HP. K 1 row to Rt, bring 1 N to HP. Cont to bring 1 N to HP on each row until 18(18:20:20:21) Ns to Rt centre are in HP. K to row 84(96:96:102:110). Set for stocking st. Break yarns, thread WY, K 6 rows and remove shoulder from machine.
  Repeat this shaping for Lt shoulder reversing instructions, reading Lt for Rt. This leaves centre neck sts on machine. K 6 rows, WY across these and remove from machine.

FRONT

As for back to row 66(78:78:84:92). Set for Hold. Mark punchcard. All Ns to Lt centre and 4(4:5:5:5) to Rt in HP. K 1 row to Lt, bring 1 N to HP. K 1 row to Rt, bring 1 N to HP. Cont to bring 1 N to HP on every row until 18(18:20:20:21) Ns to Rt centre are in HP. K to row 84(96:96:102:110). Break yarns. Set for stocking st. Thread WY and K 6 rows before removing shoulder from machine. Repeat this shaping for Lt shoulder reversing instructions reading Lt for Rt etc. This leaves centre neck sts on machine. Thread WY, K 6 rows and remove from machine.

FIRST SHOULDER SEAM

Replace sts Lt shoulder back on Ns with Rt side garment facing. Pull out WY. K 1 row MY T8. Take front of garment and with Rt sides tog, place sts Lt shoulder on Ns in WP. K 1 row T8 and cast off going behind sinker gates.
  Second shoulder seam is not made until neckband has been attached.

Row 1 MY/CY1
2 MY/CY1
3 MY/CY4
4 MY/CY4
5 MY/CY2
6 MY/CY2
7 MY/CY3
8 MY/CY2
9 MY/CY2
10 MY/CY4
11 MY/CY4
12 MY/CY1
13 MY/CY1
14 MY/–
15 CY4/CY5
16 CY4/CY5
17 CY4/CY5
18 CY4/CY5
19 MY/–
20 MY/CY3
21 MY/CY3
22 MY/CY3
23 MY/CY4
24 MY/CY4
25 MY/CY1
26 MY/CY4
27 MY/CY4
28 MY/CY3
29 MY/CY3
30 MY/CY3
31 MY/–
32 MY/–

This is the pattern repeat

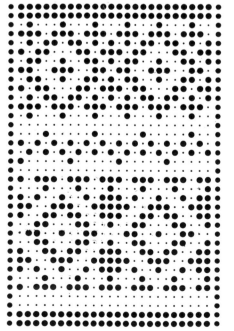

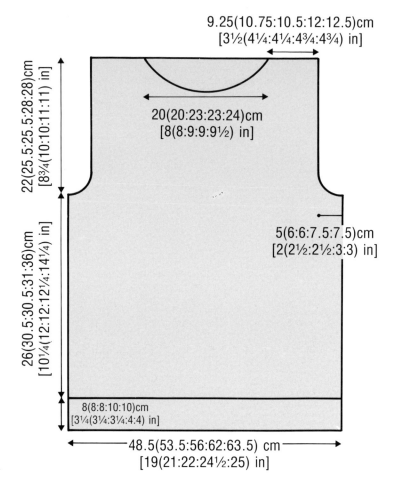

9.25(10.75:10.5:12:12.5)cm
[3½(4¼:4¼:4¾:4¾) in]

22(25.5:25.5:28:28)cm
[8¾(10:10:11:11) in]

20(20:23:23:24)cm
[8(8:9:9:9½) in]

5(6:6:7.5:7.5)cm
[2(2½:2½:3:3) in]

26(30.5:30.5:31:36)cm
[10¼(12:12:12¼:14¼) in]

8(8:8:10:10)cm
[3¼(3¼:3¼:4:4) in]

48.5(53.5:56:62:63.5) cm
[19(21:22:24½:25) in]

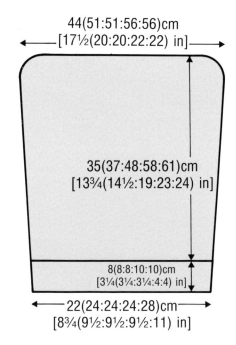

44(51:51:56:56)cm
[17½(20:20:22:22) in]

35(37:48:58:61)cm
[13¾(14½:19:23:24) in]

8(8:8:10:10)cm
[3¼(3¼:3¼:4:4) in]

22(24:24:24:28)cm
[8¾(9½:9½:9½:11) in]

NECKBAND

Using ribber cast on 82(82:88:88:90) sts in MY for 2:1 rib. T0/0 rib 16 rows. T7/7 rib 1 row. Transfer all sts to main bed. Pick up alt loops from cast on row and put back on Ns in work. K 1 row MY T8. Take main garment pieces and with Rt sides tog lay neck edge along Ns. Pick up sts on WY and replace on Ns tog with every loop and alt 'knots' from remaining neck edge (¾ of all sts). K 1 row T8 and cast off loosely going in front of sinker gates and using a claw weight to stretch st.

SLEEVE

K 2 alike. Using ribber cast on in MY 38(42:42:42:50) sts for 2:1 rib. T0/0 rib 27(27:27:29:29) rows. T7/7 rib 1 row. Transfer all sts to main bed. Carr at Rt. RC 000 set punchcard. T8 K 1 row then start Fair Isle. Inc 1 st either end of row every row for 8 rows on small, medium ladies', medium men's and large sizes, then every 2(2:4:4) rows. On extra-large size inc 1 st either end row every 4 rows throughout (78(90:90:98:98) sts.) RC 60(64:82:98:104) break yarns, thread WY, K 6 rows and remove from machine. Turn sleeve round and replace sts on same Ns with Rt side facing. Rt sides tog, pick up sts around armhole edge main garment pieces, evenly, and place on Ns in WP. K 1 row MY T8 and cast off going behind sinker gates. Make second shoulder seam before knitting second sleeve.

TO FINISH

Back st main seam from welt to cuff. Slip st cuffs, welts and neckband. Sew in ends. Wash garment according to yarn manufacturer's recommendations.

MEN'S ALL-OVER PATTERNED JERSEY

TO FIT

Small: 91–97cm (36–38in)
across chest 53.5cm (21in)
finished length 64cm (25¼in)
sleeve length, underarm 50cm
(20in)

Medium: 97–102cm (38–40in)
across chest 61cm (24in)
finished length 69cm (27in)
sleeve length, underarm 56cm
(22in)

Large: 107–112cm (42–44in)
across chest 61cm (24in)
finished length 71cm (28in)
sleeve length, underarm 61cm
(24in)

10cm (4in) allowance for ease

YARN

250g each of Shetland wool in
winter green and lovat blue and
500g navy blue lambswool (1 end
of each makes MY)
500g bleach white Shetland wool
(use 2 ends) and 250g white
lambswool (use 1 end) (tog these
make CY)
Nethy Products, Kirkshaws Road,
Coatbridge, Scotland ML5 4SL

TENSION

Measured over Fair Isle
T8 19 sts/16.5 rows = 10cm (4in)

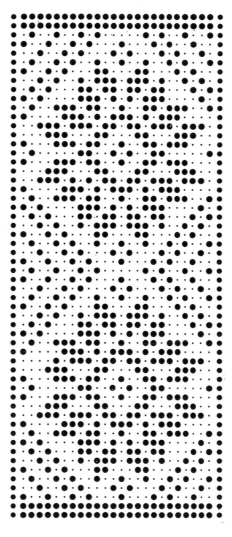

Please read pattern through
carefully before starting to knit.

BACK

Using ribber cast on 102(106:114)
sts in MY plus knit-in elastic for 2:1
rib. Remove knit-in elastic after 1st
4 rows. T0/0 rib 25 rows, T7/7 rib 1
row. Transfer all sts to main bed.
Carr at Rt RC 000 insert punchcard.
K 1 row MY T8 then start pattern.
RC 54(60:72) using 1 end of
contrast yarn, mark end st on either
side of work.
 RC 88(98:114) carr at Rt mark
punchcard. Set for Hold. All Ns to
Lt centre and 16(20:20) to Rt in
HP. K 1 row, bring 1 more N to HP.
K 1 row, bring 1 N to HP, etc until
19(23:23) Ns to Rt centre are in
HP. K. RC 92(102:118), break MY
and CY. Set for stocking st. Thread
WY, K 6 rows and remove shoulder
from machine. Repeat shaping for
Lt shoulder reversing instructions
and reading Lt for Rt. Centre neck
sts remain on machine. Thread WY,
K 6 rows and remove from
machine.

FRONT

As for back to RC 76(86:102). Carr
at Rt, set for Hold. Mark punchcard.
All Ns to Lt centre and 8(10:10) to
Rt in HP. K 1 row, bring 1 N to HP.
K 1 row, bring 1 N to HP, etc until
19(23:23) Ns are in HP. K to row
92(102:118) in pattern. Break MY

and CY. Thread WY, set for stocking st, K 6 rows and remove shoulder from machine. Repeat this shaping for Lt shoulder, reversing instructions and reading Lt for Rt. Centre neck sts remain on machine. Thread WY, K 6 rows and remove from machine.

FIRST SHOULDER SEAM

With Rt side of work facing, replace sts Lt shoulder on machine. K 1 row MY T8. Take back garment and with Rt sides tog, replace sts Lt shoulder on those already on machine. K 1 row T8. Cast off loosely.

NECKBAND

Using ribber and MY cast on 82(96:96) sts for 2:1 rib. T0/0 rib 19 rows, T7/7 rib 1 row. Transfer all sts to main bed. Pick up alt loops from cast on row and put back on Ns in work. K 1 row T8. Take main garment pieces and with Rt sides tog lay neck edge along Ns. Pick up sts on WY and replace on Ns tog with every loop and alt 'knots' from remaining neck edge (¾ of all sts). K 1 row T8 and cast off loosely.

Work second shoulder as first.

SLEEVE

Knit 2 alike. Using ribber and MY plus knit-in elastic, cast on 52(52:58) sts for 2:1 rib. T0/0 rib 25 rows, taking the knit-in elastic out after 3 rows as before. T7/7 rib 1 row. Transfer all sts to main bed. RC 000 carr at Rt. Set punchcard. K 1 row T8, start pattern. Inc 1 st either end row every other row 5 times (10 sts), then 1 st either end of row every 4 rows 13(19:19) times. RC 70(70:88), break MY and CY. Set for stocking st. Thread WY, K 6 rows and remove from machine.

Turn work round so that Rt side is facing and replace on Ns. Pull out WY. K 1 row T8 MY. Take main garment pieces and with Rt sides tog pick up sts between markers evenly along armhole edge, replacing on Ns in work. K 1 row T8 and cast off going behind sinker gates.

TO MAKE UP

Back st main seam from wrist to waist, using MY. Slip st cuffs and welts. Sew in ends, weaving them back along row of same colour. Wash garment according to yarn manufacturer's instructions (see page 12).

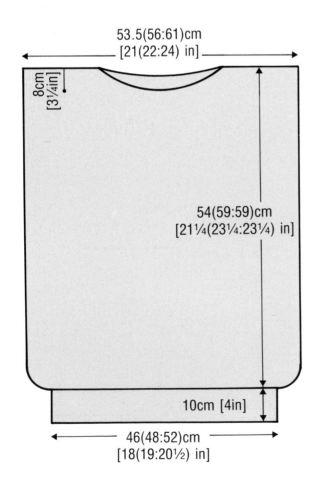

53.5(56:61)cm
[21(22:24) in]

8cm [3¼in]

54(59:59)cm
[21¼(23¼:23¼) in]

10cm [4in]

46(48:52)cm
[18(19:20½) in]

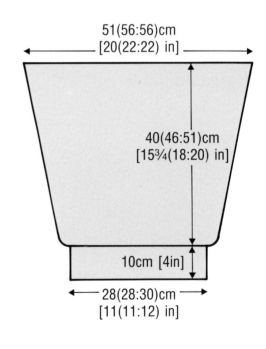

51(56:56)cm
[20(22:22) in]

40(46:51)cm
[15¾(18:20) in]

10cm [4in]

28(28:30)cm
[11(11:12) in]

Long floral jersey
Sailor-collar boxy jersey
Men's and ladies' cabled sweater

COTTON

Lace and Fair Isle jersey
Long lean tuck-stitch jersey
Ladies' waistcoat

LONG FLORAL JERSEY

TO FIT

Loose fit

Small: 87–97cm (34–38in)
across chest 60cm (23½in)
finished length 68cm (26¾in)
sleeve length from dropped
shoulder 39.5cm (15½in)

Large: 102–112cm (40–44in)
across chest 68cm (26¾in)
finished length 68cm (26¾in)
sleeve length from dropped
shoulder 39.5cm (15½in)

YARN

MY – 500g black cotton DK
CY – 500g cream cotton DK
   A. C. Wood (speciality fibres)
   Ltd, Mohair Mills, Gibson Street,
   Bradford BD3 9TS

TENSION

T8 for Fair Isle throughout
16.5 sts/16 rows = 10cm (4in)
T4 for stocking st and hems
19 sts/18 rows = 10cm (4in)

Please read pattern through
carefully before starting to knit.

BACK

Cast on 82(96) sts over every N
using WY. T8 CY K 1 row. T3 K 3
rows and pick up 1st row of loops,
putting them on same Ns. K 2 rows
MY. K 4 rows T3 CY and pick up 1st
row of loops. K 4 rows MY T4, then
start punchcard. K 18 rows MY in
feeder 1, CY in feeder 2. Stop
punchcard and K 4 rows MY T4, K 4
rows CY T3, then pick up 1st row of
loops. K 2 rows MY T4, K 4 rows CY

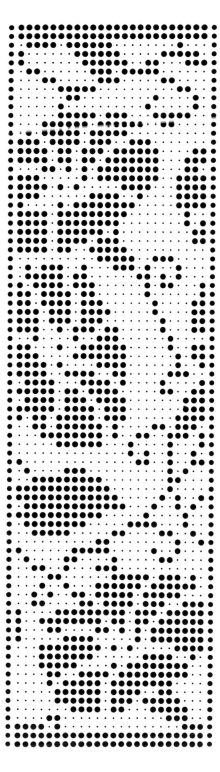

T3 and pick up 1st row of loops.
   RC 000 T8 start punchcard at
row 1. Inc 1 st at either edge of
work every 5 rows to 100(112) sts.
   RC 44 using contrast yarn place
marker at Lt and Rt edges of work.
   RC 80 mark punchcard, carr at
Rt, all Ns at Lt centre and 17 to Rt
in HP. K 1 row, then bring 1 N to
HP. K 1 row, bring 1 N to HP, etc
until 20 Ns to Rt centre are in HP.
RC 84 carr at Rt, break MY, thread
WY, K 6 rows and remove shoulder
from machine.
   Repeat this shaping for Lt
shoulder reading Rt for Lt and vice
versa. Centre neck sts remain on
machine. K 6 rows WY and remove.

FRONT

As for back to row 16. Carr at Rt,
using contrast yarn, K 16 sts at Lt
of work, starting at st 16, and 16 sts
at Rt of work, starting at st 48, by
hand, always counting from Lt.
Leave these sts on WY and
continue in Fair Isle.
   RC 44 using WY place marker at
Lt and Rt edge of work.
   RC 68 shape neck as follows:
mark punchcard, carr at Rt, all Ns
to Lt centre and 6 to Rt in HP. K 1
row then bring 1 N to HP. K 1 row,
bring 1 N to HP, etc until 20 Ns to
Rt centre are in HP. K to row 84.
Break MY, thread WY, K 6 rows and
remove from machine. Repeat this
shaping for Lt shoulder, reading Rt
for Lt and vice versa. Centre neck
sts remain on machine. K 6 rows
WY and remove.

FIRST SHOULDER SEAM

With Rt side back facing replace sts
Lt shoulder on Ns and pull out WY.

K 1 row MY T8. Take front and with Rt sides tog, place sts Lt shoulder on same Ns. K 1 row T8. Cast off going behind sinker gates.

NECKBAND

With wrong side garment facing, pick up all sts on WY tog with ¾ those that remain along neck edge, and replace on Ns. Pull out WY. K 1 row CY T4, then 3 rows T3 and pick up 1st row loops CY. K 4 rows MY T4, 4 rows CY T3, then pick up 1st row loops MY. K 1 row T8 and cast off loosely, going in front of sinker gates and using a claw weight hung below st to stretch st.

Second shoulder seam as first.

POCKETS

With wrong side of front facing, pick up sts at top WY and K 20 rows T4 MY. Pick up sts of garment, K 1 row T8 and cast off. Pull out WY and put sts back on Ns with wrong side work facing. K 1 row T4 CY and 3 rows T3 CY, then pick up 1st row loops. K 2 rows MY T4, K 4 rows CY T3 and pick up 1st row loops CY. Cast off. Repeat for 2nd pocket.

SLEEVE

K 2 alike. Using WY cast on over every N 42 sts. K 1 row CY T8 then 3 rows T3. Pick up 1st row loops CY. K 2 rows MY T4. K 4 rows T3 CY and pick up 1st row loops CY. K 4 rows MY T4, then start punchcard. K 18 rows MY in feeder 1, CY in feeder 2. Stop punchcard. K 4 rows MY T4. K 4 rows CY T3, then pick up 1st row loops CY. K 2 rows MY T4, K 4 rows CY T3 and pick up 1st row loops as before.

RC 000 T8 start punchcard at row 001. Inc 1 st at either end row every 2 rows to 82 sts. RC 40 stop punchcard. K 4 rows T3 CY, then pick up 1st row of loops and place on Ns again. K 2 rows MY and repeat. Finish 1 row MY T8. Thread WY, K 6 rows and remove from machine. Turn sleeve round so that Rt side is facing and replace sts on Ns. Take main garment piece and match shoulder seam to centre 0, markers to Lt and Rt edge sleeve. Pick up sts evenly along edge garment. K 1 row T8 and cast off loosely, going in front of sinker gates as before.

TO MAKE UP

Mattress st cuffs, welts and neckband on outside, to match pattern. Back st main seam from cuff to welt. Sew in ends. Steam press.

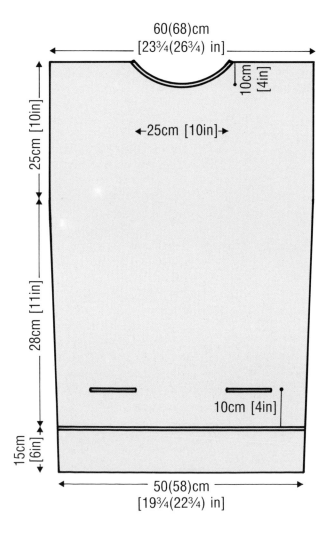

60(68)cm [23¾(26¾) in]
10cm [4in]
25cm [10in]
←25cm [10in]→
28cm [11in]
10cm [4in]
15cm [6in]
50(58)cm [19¾(22¾) in]

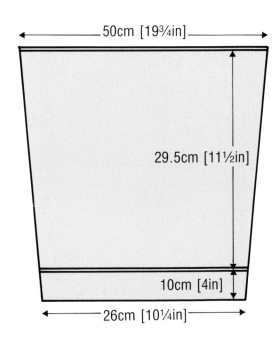

50cm [19¾in]
29.5cm [11½in]
10cm [4in]
26cm [10¼in]

SAILOR-COLLAR BOXY JERSEY

TO FIT

Small: 82–87cm (32–34in)
across chest 46cm (18in)
finished length 40cm (16in)
sleeve length 43cm (17in)

Medium: 92–97cm (36–38in)
across chest 51cm (20in)
finished length 45cm (18in)
sleeve length 43cm (17in)

Large: 102–107cm (40–42in)
across chest 58cm (23in)
finished length 45cm (18in)
sleeve length 45cm (18in)

YARN

MY – 2 cones (1kg) -21 navy blue;
CY – 50g -01 cream cotton DK
A. C. Wood (speciality fibres)
Ltd, Mohair Mills, Gibson Street,
Bradford BD3 9TS

BUTTONS: 7

TENSION

Measured over stocking st T4 : 17
sts/21 rows = 10cm (4in)

Please read pattern through
carefully before starting to knit.

BACK

Using ribber cast on 78(86:98) sts
in MY for 2:1 rib. T3/3 rib 10 rows.
Change to CY and rib 2 rows.
Transfer all sts to main bed. RC 000
T4 K MY 20(30:30) rows. Carr at Rt
cast off 8 sts at carr side. K 1 row
then cast off 8 sts at carr side. Cont

to K in stocking st to RC 72(82:82).
Shape back neck using HP. Carr at
Rt all Ns to Lt centre and 10(10:16)
to Rt in HP. K 1 row, bring 1 N to
HP. K 1 row and cont to bring 1 N
to HP on each row until 15(15:20)
Ns to Rt centre are in HP. RC
78(88:88), break MY, thread WY, K
6 rows and remove shoulder from
machine. Repeat this shaping for Lt
shoulder reading Lt for Rt and vice
versa. Centre neck sts remain on
machine. Thread WY, K 6 rows and
remove.

FRONT

Using ribber cast on 36(40:46) sts
in MY for 2:1 rib. T3/3 rib 10 rows.
Change to CY and rib 2 rows.
Transfer all sts to main bed.
    RC 000 carr at Rt T4 K MY to
row 20(30:30). Cast off 8 sts at carr
side. K to row 58(68:68). Carr at Rt
shape neck using HP. Bring 6 Ns at
Lt edge of work to HP and K 1 row.
Bring 1 N to HP on this and every
row until 12(12:18) Ns at Lt edge
are in HP. K. RC 78(88:88), break
MY, thread WY, K 6 rows and
remove shoulder from machine.
Centre neck sts remain on machine.
Set for stocking st, thread WY, K 6
rows and remove.
    Second front as first reading Lt
for Rt and vice versa.

FIRST SHOULDER SEAM

With Rt side of garment facing,
replace sts Lt shoulder front on
machine. Pull out WY. K 1 row MY
T4. Take back and place sts Lt
shoulder on Ns in work, Rt sides

tog. K 1 row T4 and cast off. Repeat
for second shoulder seam.

SLEEVE

Using ribber cast on 40(40:42) sts
in MY for 2:1 rib. T3/3 rib 10 rows.
Change to CY and rib 2 rows.
Transfer all sts to main bed.
    RC 000 T4, MY K inc 1 st either
end row every 4 rows to 84 sts. RC
86(86:90), break MY, thread WY, K
6 rows and remove from machine.
Turn sleeve round and replace sts
on Ns. K 1 row T4. Take garment
piece and pick up sts evenly along
armhole edge replacing them on Ns
with shoulder seam at centre. K 1
row T4 and cast off going behind
sinker gates.
    Second sleeve as first.

COLLAR : BACK

Using ribber cast on in MY 84 sts
for 2:1 rib. T3/3 rib 8 rows MY, then
2 rows CY. At the same time dec 1
st either end row every 2 rows.
When rib is complete, transfer all
sts to main bed. RC 000 cont to K
in MY dec as before. RC 36, shape
back neck : all Ns to Lt centre and
10(10:16) to Rt in HP. Bring 1 more
N to HP on each row until
15(15:20) Ns to Rt centre are in
HP. RC 42, remove remaining sts on
WY.
    Repeat this shaping for Lt side
collar, cont to dec at Lt edge as
above and reversing instructions.
Centre neck sts remain on machine.
Thread WY, K 6 rows and remove
from machine.

COLLAR : FRONT

Using ribber cast on 40 sts in MY for 2:1 rib. T3/3 rib 8 rows then 2 rows CY. At the same time dec 1 st at Rt edge every 2 rows. When rib is complete transfer all sts to main bed and cont to dec (MY). RC 22, start neck shaping using HP. Bring 6 Ns at Lt edge into HP then 1 each row until 12(12:18) Ns at Lt in HP. K to row 42. Break MY, thread WY, K 6 rows across these sts and remove from machine.

Repeat for opposite front reading Lt for Rt, etc.

COLLAR : SIDE

Using ribber cast on 60 sts in MY for 2:1 rib. T3/3 rib 8 rows then 2 rows CY. At the same time dec 1 st either end row every row. When rib is complete, transfer all sts to main bed and cont to K in MY dec as above until no sts left.

TO ATTACH COLLAR

Replace sts main garment piece on WY on machine with wrong side work facing. Take collar and with wrong sides tog replace sts on WY and those that remain round neck edge on Ns in WP. Pull out WY. K 1 row T4 and cast off going behind sinker gates.

Note that collar seams may be slip-stitched before making this seam if preferred.

FRONT COLLAR EDGE

Using ribber cast on 18 sts in MY for 2:1 rib. K 4 rows T3/3. Transfer all sts to main bed. Lay edge of front collar along these sts and pick up evenly. K 1 row T4 and cast off.
 Repeat for second front collar edge.

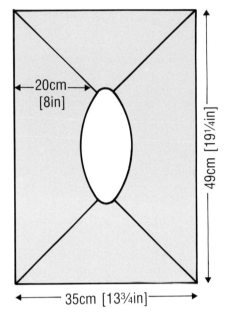

FRONT BANDS

Using ribber cast on 52(60:60) sts in MY for 2:1 rib. T3/3 rib 10 rows. Transfer all sts to main bed. K 1 row T4. Take 1 front garment and lay along band. Pick up sts on edge of garment evenly. K 1 row by hand casting off each st as you do so.
 Second band As above but make buttonholes by transferring 1 st from top to bottom bed, and 1 from bottom to top on row 6 every 11th st. Make sure that there is a hole at either end of band.

TO MAKE UP

Mattress st or slip st edges of collar, making sure that cream stripe matches at corners. Back st main seam from welt to cuff. Slip st cuffs and welts. Sew in cnds. Sew on buttons. Steam press.

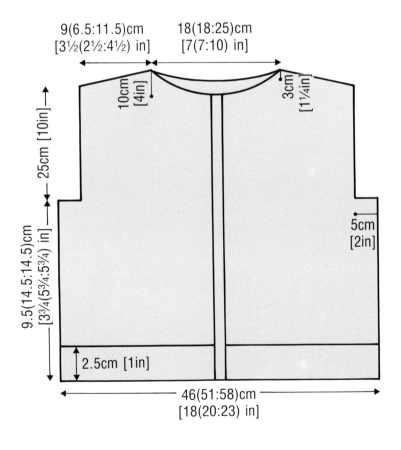

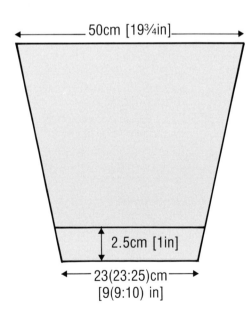

MEN'S AND LADIES' CABLED SWEATER

TO FIT

Small: 82–87cm (32–34in)
across chest 51cm (20in)
finished length 64cm (25¼in)
sleeve length 43cm (17in)

Medium (ladies'): 92–97cm (36–38in)
across chest 56cm (22in)
finished length 68.5cm (27in)
sleeve length 45cm (17¾in)

Medium (men's): 97–102cm (38–40in)
across chest 58.5cm (23in)
finished length 69cm (27¼in)
sleeve length 56cm (22in)

Large: 107–112cm (42–44in)
across chest 63.5cm (25in)
finished length 69cm (27¼in)
sleeve length 66cm (26in)

15cm (6in) allowance for ease

YARN

1kg cream or navy cotton DK
A. C. Wood (speciality fibres)
Ltd, Mohair Mills, Gibson Street,
Bradford BD3 9TS

TENSION

Measured over pattern, T4
17 sts/26 rows = 10cm (4in)

Cables: (6 st panel)
Cross sts 3 and 4 over sts 1 and 2. K 2 rows. Cross sts 3 and 4 over sts 5 and 6. K 2 rows. These 4 rows form the pattern. Before knitting 2nd row each time, bring Ns from NWP to WP and K. Return empty Ns to NWP. This creates extra yarn for twisting the cable.
Lace: as chart. 6 rows between each motif.

Please read pattern through carefully before starting to knit.

BACK

Using ribber cast on 86(96:100:108) sts in MY + knit-in elastic for 2:1 rib. T0/0 rib 34 rows (remove knit-in elastic after 1st 4 rows). Transfer all sts to main bed. RC 000 working from centre outwards, transfer 2nd, 9th, 21st, 28th, 31st, etc sts to adjacent Ns. These empty Ns remain in NWP throughout.
Carr at Rt T4 K 2 rows, start cable, start lace. K in pattern to row 84(86:88:86). Carr at Rt. Cast off 5(6:6:8) sts at carr side. K 1 row, cast off 5(6:6:8) sts at carr side. Cont in pattern dec 1 st at carr side on next and every row until 8(10:10:13) sts have been dec either side all tog. K in pattern to row 134(146:148:150). Shape back neck as follows, using HP : all Ns to Lt centre and 16(16:10:10) to Rt in HP. K 1 row. Bring 1 N to HP, K 1 row, etc until 21(21:15:15) Ns to Rt centre are in HP. K to row 140(152:154:154). Latch up cables. Break MY, thread WY, K 6 rows and remove shoulder from machine. Repeat shaping for Lt shoulder, reversing instructions and reading Rt for Lt and vice versa.
Centre neck sts remain on machine. Using WY, K 6 rows and remove from machine.

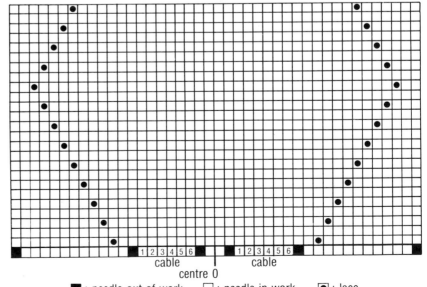

cable   cable
centre 0

■ : needle out of work   □ : needle in work   ⊡ : lace

41

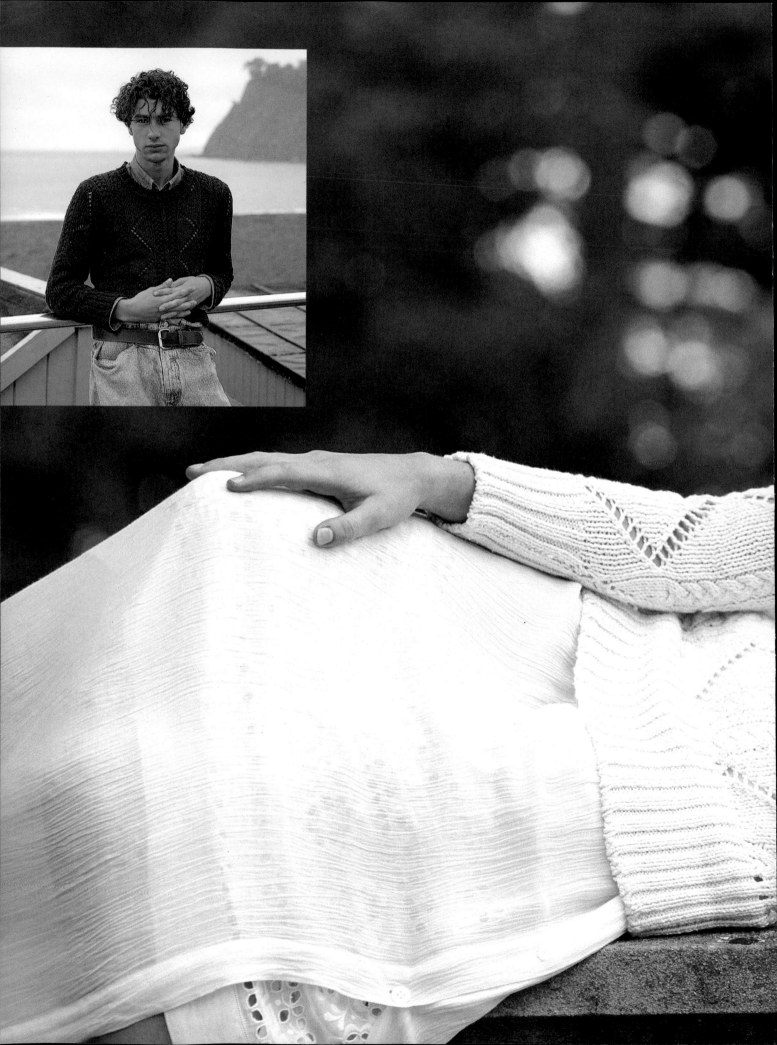

FRONT

As for back to row 114(126:128:130). Carr at Rt, shape front neck using HP. All Ns to Lt centre in HP and 6 to Rt. K 1 row, bring 2 Ns to HP. K 1 row, bring 2 Ns to HP. K 1 row, bring 1 N to HP. Cont bringing 1 N to HP each row until 21(21:15:15) Ns to Rt centre are in HP. K to row 140(152:154:156). Latch up cables. Break MY, thread WY, K 6 rows and remove from machine.

Repeat this shaping for Lt shoulder reversing instructions and reading Lt for Rt and vice versa. Centre neck sts remain on machine. Break MY, thread WY, K 6 rows and remove from machine.

FIRST SHOULDER SEAM

With Rt side garment facing you, replace sts Lt shoulder on machine.

K 1 row T4. Take back garment and with Rt sides tog replace sts Lt shoulder on Ns in work. Pull out WY. K 1 row MY T4 and cast off going behind sinker gates.

NECKBAND

Using ribber cast on 104(104:84:84) sts in MY for 2:1 rib. T0/0 rib 10 rows, then transfer all sts to main bed. K 1 row T4. Take main garment pieces and lay along neckband. Pick up evenly along garment edge, including sts on WY. K 1 row T4 and cast off loosely.

Work second shoulder as first.

SLEEVES

K 2 alike. Using ribber cast on 40(40:48:48) sts in MY + knit-in elastic for 2:1 rib. T0/0 rib 34 rows. Remove knit-in elastic. Transfer all

sts to main bed. RC 000 working from centre outwards, transfer 2nd, 9th, 21st, etc sts to adjacent Ns, as diagram. Carr at Rt T4 K 2 rows. Start cable, start lace. Inc 1 st either end of row every other row for 10 rows, then every 6(4:7:7) rows to 74(86:86:94) sts. RC 78(82:112:133). Dec 1 st either end of row 3(4:4:5) times, then cast off 5(6:6:8) sts at carr side. K 1 row and repeat. Latch up cables. Remove remaining sts on WY as usual.

TO MAKE UP

Turn sleeve round and replace sts on WY on Ns with Rt side of work facing you. With Rt sides tog, place main garment piece against sleeve and pick up sts evenly along edge. K 1 row T4 and cast off.

Back st main seam from cuff to welt. Slip st cuffs and welts. Wash.

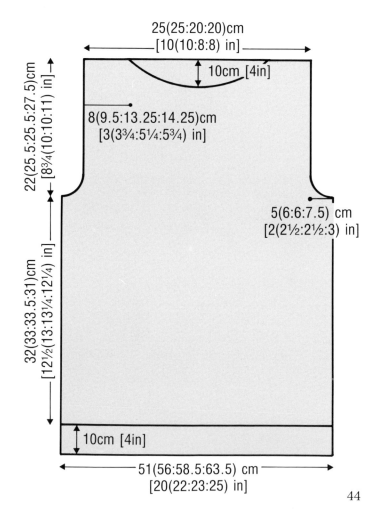

25(25:20:20)cm
[10(10:8:8) in]

10cm [4in]

8(9.5:13.25:14.25)cm
[3(3¾:5¼:5¾) in]

22(25.5:25.5:27.5)cm
[8¾(10:10:11) in]

5(6:6:7.5) cm
[2(2½:2½:3) in]

32(33:33.5:31)cm
[12½(13:13¼:12¼) in]

10cm [4in]

51(56:58.5:63.5) cm
[20(22:23:25) in]

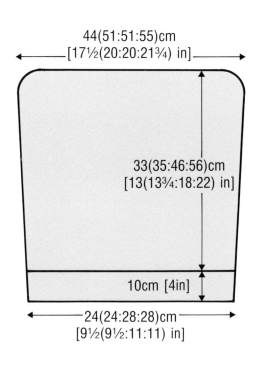

44(51:51:55)cm
[17½(20:20:21¾) in]

33(35:46:56)cm
[13(13¾:18:22) in]

10cm [4in]

24(24:28:28)cm
[9½(9½:11:11) in]

LACE AND FAIR ISLE JERSEY

TO FIT

Small: 81–87cm (32–34in)
across chest 53cm (21in)
finished length 56cm (22in)
sleeve length 43cm (17in)

Medium: 92–97cm (36–38in)
across chest 58.5cm (23in)
finished length 58.5cm (23in)
sleeve length 46cm (18in)

Large: 102–107cm (40–42in)
across chest 64cm (25in)
finished length 64cm (25in)
sleeve length 48.5cm (19in)

Extra large: 112–122cm (44–48in)
across chest 66cm (26in)
finished length 69cm (27in)
sleeve length 51cm (20in)

YARN

a) MY – 2 cones cream cotton DK
   CY1 – 100g sage green cotton DK
   CY2 – 50g silver beige cotton DK
   CY3 – 50g taupe cotton DK

b) MY – 2 cones navy blue cotton DK
   CY1 – 100g mauve cotton DK
   CY2 – 50g purple cotton DK
   CY3 – 50g lead blue cotton DK
   A. C. Wood (speciality fibres) Ltd, Mohair Mills, Gibson Street, Bradford BD3 9TS.

TENSION

T4 measured over lace and Fair Isle. 17 sts/21 rows = 10cm (4in)

Note: This pattern relies mainly on hand-tooling, together with an 8-row Fair Isle pattern, and so could easily be achieved on one of the more basic machines such as the Bond. A little practice at hand selection of Ns for Fair Isle is all that is necessary.

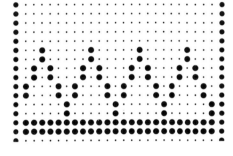

Please read pattern through carefully before starting to knit.

BACK

Cast on 90(100:108:112) sts in MY + knit-in elastic for 2:1 rib. T0/0 rib 4 rows then remove knit-in elastic before continuing. Rib 30(30:36:36) rows all tog, then transfer all sts to main bed.

RC 000 MY T4 K 4 rows
* Make 1st row holes for lace (see chart)
K 2 rows CY1, make 2nd row holes
K 2 rows CY2, make 3rd row holes
K 2 rows CY2, make 4th row holes
K 4 rows MY, make 1st row holes
K 2 rows MY, make 2nd row holes
K 2 rows MY, make 3rd row holes
K 2 rows MY, make 4th row holes
K 1 row MY, then set punchcard ready for Fair Isle. Set carr to read punchcard. K 1 row MY. Start Fair Isle, CY3 in feeder 2. K 6 rows.
Break MY and thread CY1 in feeder 1. CY3 remains in feeder 2. K 2 rows. Remove punchcard. K 2 rows CY2. K 6 rows MY. * Pattern repeats from * to *.
K in pattern to row 100(106:112:122). Carr at Rt. Shape back neck while continuing in pattern as follows : set carr for Hold, all Ns to Lt centre in HP and 12 to Rt. *Note:* if your machine does not have a HP, take the appropriate number of sts back to

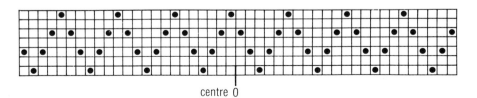

centre 0

☐ : needle in work
◉ : lace

45

NWP using the nylon cord. K 1 row, then bring 1 N to HP. K 1 row, bring 1 N to HP, etc until 17 Ns to Rt centre are in HP. Finish at row 106(112:118:128). Break yarn, thread WY and K 6 rows. Remove shoulder from machine. Repeat this shaping for Lt shoulder, reading Rt for Lt and vice versa. Centre sts remain on machine.

Thread WY, K 6 rows and remove from machine.

FRONT

As for back to row 84(90:96:108). Carr at Rt, shape neck as follows: continuing to knit in pattern, bring all Ns to Lt centre to HP and 7 to Rt. Set carr for Hold. K 1 row, bring 1 N to HP. K 1 row, bring 1 N to HP, etc until 17 Ns are in HP to Rt centre. K in pattern to row 106(112:118:128). Break yarn. Thread WY, K 6 rows and remove shoulder from machine. Repeat shaping for Lt shoulder reversing instructions. Centre sts remain on

machine. Thread WY, K 6 rows and remove from machine.

SHOULDER SEAM

With Rt side garment facing you, replace sts Lt shoulder on machine. Take back garment and with Rt sides tog replace sts Lt shoulder on Ns in work. Pull out WY. K 1 row MY T4 and cast off going behind sinker gates. Repeat for second shoulder seam.

SLEEVE

K 2 alike. Cast on 48(48:51:51) sts in MY for 2:1 rib. Use knit-in elastic for 1st 4 rows as before. T0/0 rib 30(30:36:36) rows. Transfer all sts to main bed.

RC 000 K in MY T4 in pattern as before inc 1 st at either end of row every 7(7:5:5) rows. RC 78(84:86:90) cast off loosely, going in front of sinker gates and using a claw weight hung below cast off st to stretch st.

COLLAR

Using ribber cast on 86 sts in MY for 2:1 rib. T2/2 rib 30 rows. Transfer all sts to main bed. K 1 row T8 MY. Take main garment piece and pick up 1st neck edge s placing it on 1st st of collar (centr front of garment). Using long end MY make a st and cast off loosely. Go on to next st, etc until the 2 ends of the collar meet at centre front of garment.

TO MAKE UP

Back st sleeve head to shoulder edge of garment making sure underarms match and centre of sleeve head is at shoulder seam. This will need pinning first. Pin main seam from wrist to waist an back st firmly. Slip st cuffs and welts. Sew in ends of pattern colours, etc. *Note* Pins are more effective if put in at Rt angles to seam.

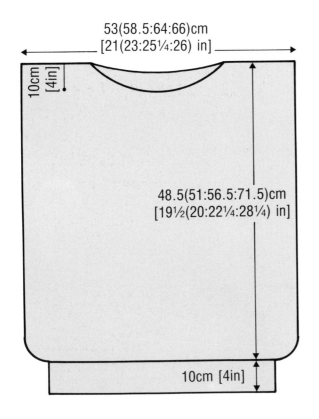

53(58.5:64:66)cm
[21(23:25¼:26) in]

10cm [4in]

48.5(51:56.5:71.5)cm
[19½(20:22¼:28¼) in]

10cm [4in]

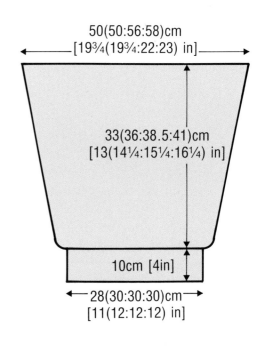

50(50:56:58)cm
[19¾(19¾:22:23) in]

33(36:38.5:41)cm
[13(14¼:15¼:16¼) in]

10cm [4in]

28(30:30:30)cm
[11(12:12:12) in]

LONG LEAN TUCK-STITCH JERSEY

TO FIT

Small: 82–87cm (32–34in)
across chest 54cm (21¼in)
finished length 73cm (28¾in)
sleeve length 49.5cm (19½in)

Medium: 92–97cm (36–38in)
across chest 56.5cm (22¼in)
finished length 75.5cm (29½in)
sleeve length 51.75cm (20½in)

Large: 102–107cm (40–42in)
across chest 59cm (23¼in)
finished length 78cm (30¾in)
sleeve length 53cm (21in)

Extra large: 112–117cm (44-46in)
across chest 62cm (24½in)
finished length 80.5cm (31¾in)
sleeve length 54.5cm (21½in)

20cm (8in) allowance for ease

YARN

2(3:3:3) cones pale pink cotton DK
  100% mercerised (colour number
  CM273)
  Texere Yarns, College Mill,
  Barkerend Road, Bradford, West
  Yorkshire BD3 9AQ

TENSION

Measured over tuck st T3
23 rows/15 sts = 10cm (4in)

Please read pattern through
carefully before starting to knit.

BACK

Using ribber cast on 85(89:93:98)
sts in MY + knit-in elastic for 2:1
rib. Rib 45 rows T0/0. Rib 1 row T3/
3. (Remove knit-in elastic after 1st
4 rows.) Transfer all sts to main
bed. Break MY, K 6 rows WY and
remove from machine. Replace
these sts on 81(85:88:94) Ns,
placing 2 sts on the same N, 4
times, at even intervals across the
work. Carr at Rt.
  RC 000 K 1 row T3. Set
punchcard and carr for tuck st. K

Punchcard no.8P from Jones/
Brother basic pack

90(94:100:106) rows. Carr at Rt
cast off 5(7:7:8) sts at carr side. K 1
row, cast off 5(7:7:8) sts at carr
side. Continue in tuck st, casting off
1 st at carr side on next and
following 3 rows. 7(9:9:10) sts in all
at either edge. K in tuck st to row
150(154:174:186). Carr at Rt, mark
punchcard.
  All Ns to Lt centre and 14 to Rt
in HP. Set for Hold. K 1 row. Bring
1 N to HP. K 1 row and repeat until
19 Ns to Rt centre are in HP. At
row 156(160:180:192) break yarn.
Thread WY K 6 rows and remove
from machine. Repeat this shaping
for Lt shoulder reading Lt for Rt.
  Centre neck sts remain on
machine. Thread WY, K 6 rows and
remove from machine.

FRONT

Using ribber cast on 85(89:93:98)
sts in MY + knit-in elastic for 2:1
rib.
  Rib 45 rows T0/0. Rib 1 row T3/3.
(Remove knit-in elastic after 1st 4
rows.) Transfer all sts to main bed.
Break MY, K 6 rows WY and remove
from machine. Replace these sts on
81(85:88:94) Ns, placing 2 sts on
the same N, 4 times, at even
intervals across the work. Carr at
Rt. RC 000 K 1 row T3. Set
punchcard for tuck and carr to
tuck. K 24 rows. Carr at Rt make
pockets: Ns 16–30 and 52–67
(small) 16–30 and 55–70
(medium) 19–34 and 55–70
(large) and 21–36 and 59–74
(extra-large) in HP. K these Ns
back to UWP by hand using WY.

This marks the pockets. Continue to K in tuck st to row 90(94:100:106). Carr at Rt cast off 5(7:7:8) sts at carr side. K 1 row. Cast off 5(7:7:8) sts. K 1 row. Cast off 1 st, K 1 row. Repeat twice then cast off 1 st.

Row 98(102:108:114) mark punchcard and shape neck as follows : all Ns to Lt centre in HP (or take Ns back NWP using nylon cord). Set for Hold and continue to K in tuck st at Rt while dec 1 st fully fashioned at Lt edge of work every 3 rows to 15(15:18:18) sts.

Row 156(160:170:172). Set for stocking st. Break MY, thread WY, K 6 rows and remove shoulder from machine. Repeat this shaping from row 98(102:108:114) reading Lt for Rt.

SHOULDER SEAM

With Rt side garment facing you, replace sts Lt shoulder on machine. Take back garment and with Rt sides tog replace sts Lt shoulder on Ns in work. Pull out WY. K 1 row MY T4 and cast off going behind sinker gates.

NECKBAND

Using ribber cast on 82 sts in MY for 2:1 rib. T0/0 rib 10 rows. Transfer all sts to main bed. K 1 row T5. Wth Rt side garment facing machine, pick up evenly along front edge and all sts on WY along back neck. K 1 row T5. Cast off loosely, going in front of sinker gates and using a claw weight hung below st being cast off, to stretch st.

The 1st piece of neckband goes across the back neck and down 1 edge of garment to point of V and the 2nd piece goes down the opposite edge neck to point of V. There is 1 seam on the shoulder.

Using ribber cast on 42 sts in MY for 2:1 rib. T0/0 rib 10 rows, etc as for 1st piece of neckband. Attach as above.

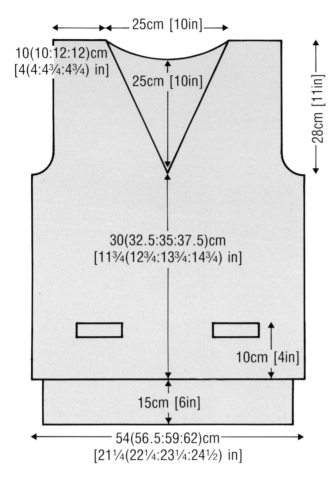

25cm [10in]

10(10:12:12)cm
[4(4:4¾:4¾) in]

25cm [10in]

28cm [11in]

30(32.5:35:37.5)cm
[11¾(12¾:13¾:14¾) in]

10cm [4in]

15cm [6in]

54(56.5:59:62)cm
[21¼(22¼:23¼:24½) in]

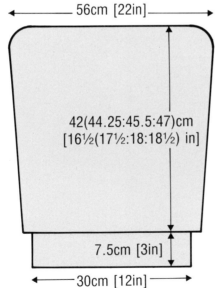

56cm [22in]

42(44.25:45.5:47)cm
[16½(17½:18:18½) in]

7.5cm [3in]

30cm [12in]

SLEEVE

K 2 alike. Using ribber cast on 46 sts in MY + knit-in elastic for 2:1 rib. T0/0 rib 26 rows (remove knit-in elastic after 1st 4 rows), then rib 1 row T3/3.

Transfer all sts to main bed. Carr at Rt. RC 000 set punchcard. K 1 row T3. Set carr to tuck and K, inc 1 st at either end row every 5th row to 84 sts. RC 93(96:98:102). Dec 1 st at either end row every row 3 times on small size. Dec 1 st at either end row every other row on medium, large and extra-large sizes. RC 96(102:104:108). Cast off going behind sinker gates.

POCKETS

Pick up sts at top of pocket on WY with wrong side garment facing and K 50 rows MY T3. K 6 rows WY.

Using ribber cast on 16 sts in MY for 2:1 rib. Rib 10 rows T3/3.

Transfer all sts to main bed. K 1 row. Replace sts top pocket and pocket lining on these Ns. K 1 row T5 and cast off loosely.

Work second shoulder seam as first.

TO MAKE UP

Please note wrong side of work is right side of garment. Back st sleeve head to armhole edge matching centre to shoulder seam. Back st main seam from cuff to welt. Slip st cuffs and welts. Slip st neckband ends. Sew in ends. Steam press if desired.

LADIES' WAISTCOAT

TO FIT

Small: 81–92cm (32–36in)
Back length 40cm (16in)

Large: 92–102cm (36–40in)
Back length 43cm (17in)

YARN

MY – 450g cone TF104 natural
  cotton bouclé DK equivalent
  Texere Yarns designer collection,
  College Mill, Barkerend Road,
  Bradford, West Yorkshire
  BD3 9AQ
CY – 100g Colinette Milan (silk and
  linen)
  Colinette Yarns, Park Lane
  House, High Street, Welshpool,
  Powys, Wales

Buttons: 5

TENSION

T1 over Fair Isle
19 sts/23 rows = 10cm (4in)
Over stocking st
18 sts/30 rows = 10cm (4in)

Note: This waistcoat is designed
to be worn next to the skin so there
is minimal allowance for ease. It is
not an overgarment.

Please read pattern through
carefully before starting to knit.

BACK

Using closed-edge method ('E-
wrap') and MY, cotton bouclé, cast
on 72(86) sts. T1 K 10 rows, dec 1
st at either end of row and on every
5th(7th) row following, to 68(82)

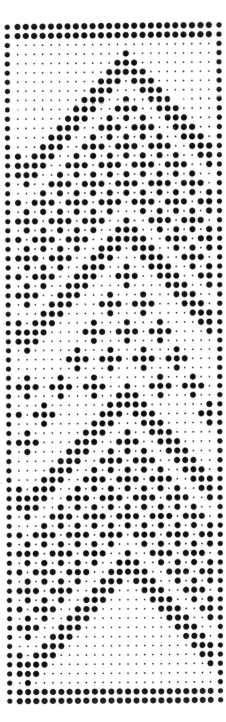

sts. K 4(6) rows. RC 30(34). Then
inc 1 st at either end of row every
6th row to 78(92) sts.
  RC 60(64). Carr at Rt. Cast off
2(4) sts, K 1 row, cast off 2(4) sts.
Small size repeat twice. Then dec 1
st at either end of row every other
row 6(4) times. 58(68) sts. RC
74(78).
  K, inc 1 st at either end of row
every 16 rows 3 times. 64(76) sts
RC 122(126).
  Shape shoulder using HP : dec
sts by bringing Ns out to HP every
other row at opposite edge of work
to carr in the following sequence :
3, 3, 2, 2, 2, 2.
At the same time when RC reads
124(129) shape back neck : all Ns
to Lt and 7(13) to Rt of centre in
HP. Cast off 7(13) sts to Lt using
spare end MY. Cast off 7(13) to Rt.
K 1 row then cast off 2 sts, followed
by 1 st every row until 25(36) sts
cast off. RC 134(138).
  Repeat this shaping for Lt
shoulder and neck edge, reversing
instructions, reading Lt for Rt and
vice versa.

FRONT

Using closed-edge method, cast on
40(45) sts in MY. T1 K 1 row. Set
for Hold. Start punchcard. CY in
feeder 2. Bring 24(28) Ns to Lt
centre and 13(17) to Rt centre,
counting inwards from outside
edge, to HP, leaving 4(5) Ns in
centre in work. K 1 row, then bring
3 Ns at opposite side to carr, to WP,
K 1 row, etc. At the Lt edge inc 3
sts 3 times, both sizes, followed by
4 sts twice (4 times). At the Rt
edge inc 2 sts once and 3 sts 4
times, small 3 sts five times, large.

RC 10(13). K straight at Rt edge cont to inc at Lt edge, as follows: 4 sts once, 3 sts once small only. RC 14.

All Ns in WP. At Lt edge only dec 1 st at row 18(23) and 1 st at row 28(33). K straight to row 36 then inc 1 st at Lt edge every 6th row to row 66(68). 5 sts in all. At Rt edge of work RC 68(72) start neck shaping : dec 1 st fully fashioned every 2 rows 19(22) times. K 2(6) rows.

At the same time at Lt edge only dec 1 st each row 4 times, then every 3 rows 8 times, small. Dec 1 st at Lt edge every 2 rows 12 times, large. K 2(6) rows. RC 96(98). K.

RC 100(104) at Lt edge inc 1 st and again at row 108(112).

RC 110(116) shape shoulder using HP. Carr at Rt. Bring 4(5) Ns at Lt to HP. K 2 rows. Repeat this twice, then large size, 2 sts once. When all shoulder Ns are in HP break CY, set for stocking st K 1 row T1 MY. Break MY, thread up WY, K 6 rows and remove from machine.

Knit Rt front as Lt, reversing all shapings, reading Lt for Rt and vice versa.

TO MAKE UP

Shoulder seams Take front of garment and replace sts on WY on machine. Match shoulder back of garment, Rt sides tog, and replace sts on same Ns. K 1 row MY T1 and cast off going behind sinker gates. Repeat for second shoulder. Back st side seams.

Edging Starting at back neck Lt shoulder seam, pick up 4 sts and K 6 rows MY T1. Pick up next 4 sts and place on same Ns, K 6 rows, and repeat. This is continued all the way round the garment and ends where it started.

Front band Repeat this edging again down the front edges only, so that there are 2 rows. On the Rt edge, to form buttonholes, leave a gap between picking up the 3rd set of 4 sts and the 4th, and repeat at regular intervals along the edge (5 buttonholes).

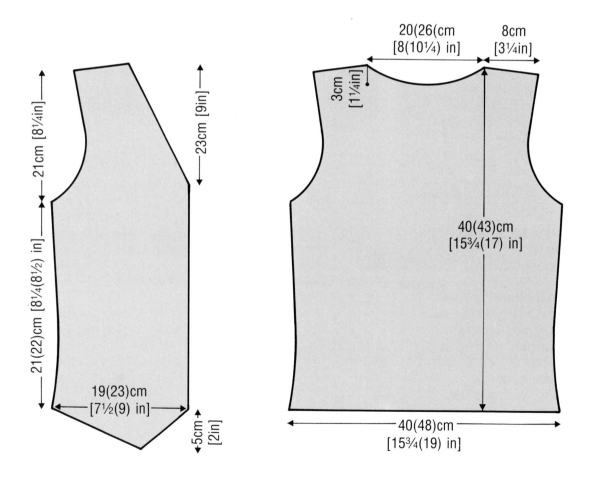

V-back cabled silk evening top

Angora evening top

EXOTIC

Silk T-shirt

Mohair and chunky silk jersey

V-BACK CABLED
SILK EVENING TOP

TO FIT

Small: 82–87cm (32–34in)
across chest 45.5cm (18in)
finished length 57cm (22½in)
sleeve underarm 44cm (17¼in)

Medium: 92–97cm (36–38in)
across chest 50.5cm (20in)
finished length 64cm (25¼in)
sleeve underarm 48cm (19in)

Large: 102–107cm (40–42in)
across chest 55.5cm (22in)
finished length 69cm (27¼in)
sleeve underarm 51cm (20in)

4cm (1½in) allowance for ease

YARN

100g pack × 100% silk in charcoal
   A. C. Wood (speciality fibres)
   Ltd, Mohair Mills, Gibson Street,
   Bradford BD3 9TS.

TENSION

T2 measured over stocking st
9 sts = 5cm (2in)
T2 measured over cables
20 sts/28 rows = 10cm (4in)

Please read pattern through
carefully before starting to knit.

NEEDLE ARRANGEMENT

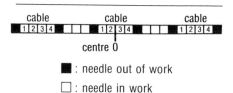

cable   cable   cable

centre 0

■ : needle out of work
□ : needle in work

FRONT

Using ribber cast on 82(90:100) sts
in MY + knit-in elastic for 2:1 rib.
T0/0 rib 34 rows, removing knit-in
elastic from feeder after 4 rows.
Transfer all sts to main bed. Break
MY, thread WY, K 6 rows and
remove from machine. Replace on
91(101:111) Ns, spacing out the
extra 9(11:11) sts at even intervals
across the work. Bring up a loop
from below the st in the row below
and place on empty N in each case.

RC 000 carr at Rt, K 1 row T2.
Transfer sts to adjacent Ns as in
chart. Cable over 4 Ns : cross sts 1
and 2 over 3 and 4 in every group
of 4 right across the bed. K 6 rows.
Repeat. Before knitting row 6 bring
empty Ns to WP. This creates extra
yarn with which to make cable.
Return to NWP before cabling.

K in pattern to row 76(86:92).
Place marker of contrast yarn at
both edges of work. K in pattern to
row 120(140:154). Latch up all sts
made by Ns in NWP. K 1 row.
Change to WY, K 6 rows and
remove from machine.

BACK

Using ribber cast on 82(90:100) sts
in MY + knit-in elastic for 2:1 rib.
T0/0 rib 34 rows, removing knit-in
elastic after 4 rows, as before.
Transfer all sts to main bed. Break
MY, thread WY, K 6 rows and
remove from machine. Replace on
91(101:111) Ns, spacing the
9(11:11) additional sts at even
intervals across the work. Bring a

loop up from below the st in the
row below and place on empty N.

RC 000 carr at Rt, K 1 row T2.
Transfer sts to adjacent Ns as in
chart. Cable as before. At row 28
take all Ns to Lt centre back to
NWP using nylon cord. Move
weights to Rt of work. Continue to
K in pattern, dec 1 st fully
fashioned at Lt edge of work every
4 rows to 15 sts. Place markers at
row 76(86:92) as before. K to row
132(150:164). Cast off.

SLEEVE

K 2 alike. Using ribber cast on
40(46:50) sts in MY + knit-in
elastic for 2:1 rib. Rib 36 rows T0/0
removing knit-in elastic after 4
rows. Transfer all sts to main bed.
Carr at Rt K 6 rows WY. Replace sts
on 44(50:54) Ns, spacing extra 4 sts
evenly across work. Bring up a loop
from below the st in the row below
and place on empty N, in each case.

RC 000 K 1 row T2. Transfer sts
to adjacent Ns as shown in chart.

Cable as before inc 1 st at either
edge of work, maintaining pattern,
every 5 rows. At row 94(105:131)
latch up sts made by empty Ns. K 1
row. Cast off loosely.

FRONT NECKBAND

Using ribber cast on 91(90:100) sts
in MY for 2:1 rib. T0/0 rib 10 rows.
Transfer all sts to main bed. K 1
row T2. Take front garment piece
and replace sts on WY on Ns in WP.
K 1 row T2 and cast off going
behind sinker gates.

BACK NECKBAND

K 2 alike. Using ribber cast on 78(92:103) sts in MY for 2:1 rib. T0/0 rib 10 rows. Transfer all sts to main bed. K 1 row T2. Take back garment and place against ribbed band, right sides tog. Pick up sts evenly along edge and replace on Ns in WP. K 1 row T2 and cast off going behind sinker gates.

Repeat for opposite neck edge.

SHOULDER SEAM

Take sleeve and replace sts on WY on machine with Rt side work facing. Take front and back of garment and with Rt sides tog, pick up sts along edge, working 2 sts in from the edge, evenly between markers. Unravel WY. K 1 row T2 and cast off behind sinker gates.

TO MAKE UP

St ends back neckbands down, beneath front band before making shoulder seams. Place sleeve head between markers right sides tog and matching centre sleeve to shoulder seam, then back st. St ends bands at point of V so that one overlaps the other. Back st main seam from cuff to welt. Slip st cuffs and welts.

Note: Those with narrow shoulders may find that, on wearing, this garment has a tendency to slip off one shoulder. In this case knit a cord, or several cords, as follows : cast on over 3 Ns using closed-edge method. Set for slip in one direction only, and K the desired number of rows. Cast off. St this across the width of the V.

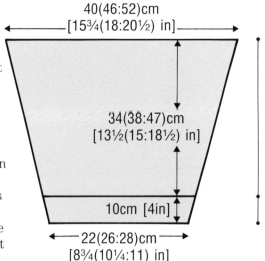

40(46:52)cm
[15¾(18:20½) in]

34(38:47)cm
[13½(15:18½) in]

10cm [4in]

22(26:28)cm
[8¾(10¼:11) in]

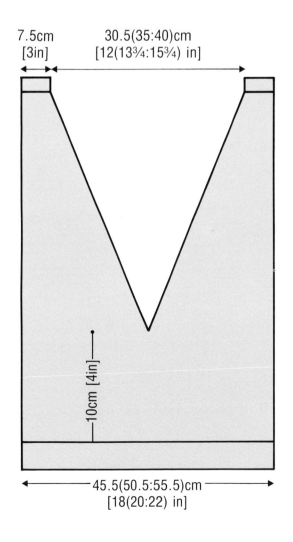

7.5cm
[3in]

30.5(35:40)cm
[12(13¾:15¾) in]

10cm [4in]

45.5(50.5:55.5)cm
[18(20:22) in]

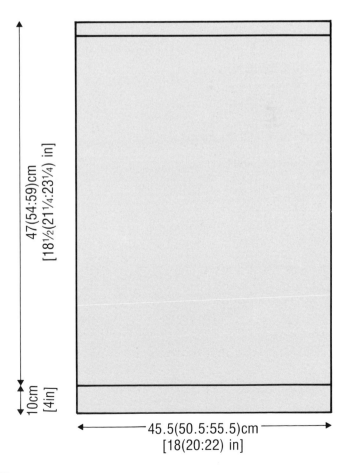

47(54:59)cm
[18½(21¼:23¼) in]

10cm
[4in]

45.5(50.5:55.5)cm
[18(20:22) in]

ANGORA EVENING TOP

TO FIT

Small: 82–87cm (32–34in)
across chest 46cm (18in)
finished length 56cm (22in)
sleeve underarm 47cm (18½in)

Medium: 92–97cm (36–38in)
across chest 51cm (20in)
finished length 64cm (25¼in)
sleeve underarm 49cm (19¼in)

Large: 102–107cm (40–42in)
across chest 56cm (22in)
finished length 69cm (27¼in)
sleeve underarm 51cm (20in)

5cm (2in) allowance for ease

YARN

240(280:340)g 100% angora in
  black (sold in 200g packs).
  A. C. Wood (speciality fibres)
  Ltd, Mohair Mills, Gibson Street,
  Bradford BD3 9TS.

TENSION

T7 : 13 sts/22 rows = 10cm (4in)

BACK

Using ribber cast on 60(66:74) sts
for 2:1 rib T0/0. Rib 14 rows. T5/5
rib 2 rows. Transfer all sts to main
bed.
  RC 000 T7 K 44(62:72) rows.
Carr at Rt. Cast off 4 sts at carr
side, K 1 row.
  Cast off 4 sts at carr side, K 1
row. Dec 1 st on next and following
alternate row (6 st all tog), at both

sides of work. K to row
84(102:112). Carr at Rt. Set for
Hold. At Lt edge shape shoulder as
follows : bring to HP 2(3:4) Ns. K 1
row to Lt, wrapping last N at Lt. K 1
row, bring 2(3:4) Ns to HP at Lt,
etc. The order in which to do this
is : small: 2, 2, 2; medium: 3, 3, 4;
large: 4, 4, 4, 4 Ns.
  Row 91(109:119) carr at Lt, all
Ns to Rt centre and 14 to Lt in HP.
  Continue shaping shoulder while
at the same time bringing 1 N to HP
at Rt edge work each row until 17
to Lt centre are in HP. When all
shoulder sts are in HP at row
95(109:118) return all Ns to UWP
and K 1 row. Break MY, thread WY,
K 6 rows and remove shoulder from
machine. Repeat this shaping for Rt
shoulder, reversing instructions,
reading Rt for Lt and vice versa.
  Centre neck sts remain on
machine. Thread WY, K 6 rows and
remove from machine.

FRONT

As for back to row 79(97:107).
  Shape front neck while shaping
shoulder as follows : carr at Lt all
Ns to Rt centre and 5 to Lt in HP. K
1 row. Bring 1 N to HP at neck
edge, K 1 row, etc until 17 Ns to Rt
centre are in HP.
  Complete as for back and repeat
shaping for Lt shoulder and neck
edge reading Rt for Lt and vice versa.

SLEEVE

K 2 alike. Using ribber cast on
28(30:31) sts for 2:1 rib. T0/0 rib 14

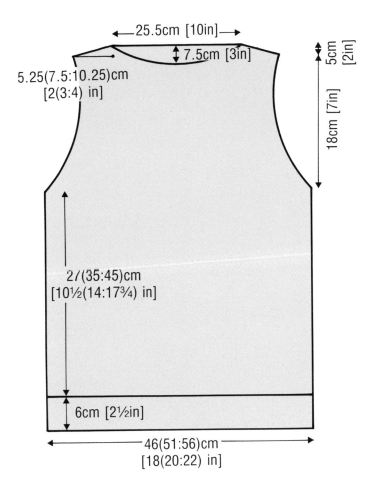

25.5cm [10in]

7.5cm [3in]

5cm [2in]

18cm [7in]

5.25(7.5:10.25)cm
[2(3:4) in]

2/(35:45)cm
[10½(14:17¾) in]

6cm [2½in]

46(51:56)cm
[18(20:22) in]

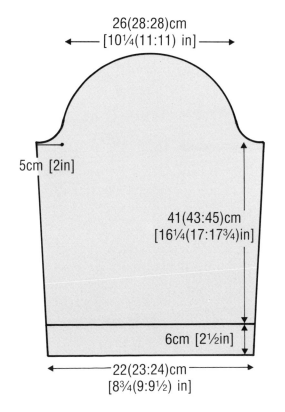

26(28:28)cm
[10¼(11:11) in]

5cm [2in]

41(43:45)cm
[16¼(17:17¾)in]

6cm [2½in]

22(23:24)cm
[8¾(9:9½) in]

rows. T5/5 rib 2 rows. Transfer all sts to main bed.

RC 000 T7 inc 1 st either end of row fully fashioned every 7(8:8) rows to 46(49:49) sts. RC 66(70:75).

Cast off 4 sts at carr side. K 1 row. Cast off 4 sts at carr side, then dec 1 st on next and following alternate row at either side (6 sts in all). Dec 1 st at either end of row every other row. RC 108(114:118). Cast off 6 remaining sts.

First shoulder seam Take back and with right side facing, replace sts Lt shoulder on machine. Take front and with right sides tog, replace sts Lt shoulder on same Ns. K 1 row T7. Cast off loosely, going in front of sinker gates and using a claw weight to stretch the st being cast off.

NECKBAND

With wrong side of garment facing, pick up sts along neck edge, including those on WY and ¾ of those that remain. K 1 row T7. K 2 rows T3. K 1 row T10. K 2 rows T3. K 1 row T7. Pick up 1st row loops and replace on Ns in work. Cast off loosely, going in front of sinker gates as before.

Second shoulder seam as first.

TO MAKE UP

Back st seam from underarm to waist. Back st sleeve seam. Slip st cuffs and welts. Turn main garment inside out and place sleeve head in armhole. Pin in place, then back st. Sew in ends.

SILK
T-SHIRT

TO FIT

Small: 82–87cm (32–34in)
across chest 48cm (19in)
finished length 48cm (19in)

Medium: 92–97cm (36–38in)
across chest 53cm (21in)
finished length 51cm (20in)

Large: 102–107cm (40–42in)
across chest 56cm (22in)
finished length 52cm (20½in)

YARN

300g spun silk 2/1s metric in pale
    blue
    J. Hyslop Bathgate & Co, Victoria
    Works, Galashiels TD1 1NY.

TENSION

T5 stocking st
17 sts/20.5 rows = 10cm (4in)

Please read pattern through
carefully before starting to knit.

BACK

Using ribber cast on 82(90:96) sts
for 1:1 rib. Rib 20 rows T0/0.
    Transfer all sts to main bed.
    RC 000 K 40(46:48) rows T5.
Carr at Rt cast off 8(10:10) sts at
carr side. K 1 row then cast off
8(10:10) sts at carr side. K 1 row
then dec 1 st at either end row
every other row 5(7:7) times. K. At
row 72(78:80) shape back neck and
shoulders as follows, using HP : carr
at Rt all Ns to Lt centre and 10 to
Rt in HP. K 1 row. Bring 2(2:3) Ns

at Rt edge work to HP. K 1 row, bring 1 N at Lt edge to HP, etc on small and medium sizes, then bring 2 Ns every row to HP; on large size bring 3:3:2:2 Ns to HP every row.

RC 82(88:90) all shoulder Ns back to WP. K 1 row. Break MY, thread WY, K 6 rows and remove. Repeat this shaping for Lt shoulder, reversing instructions and reading Lt for Rt and vice versa.

Centre neck sts remain on machine. K 1 row T5 and cast off.

FRONT

As for back to row 46(50:52). Shape front neck using HP as follows: All Ns to Lt centre in HP and 4 to Rt. K 1 row Rt to Lt, then bring 1 N to HP. K 1 row Lt to Rt, bring 1 N to HP, etc until 18 Ns to Rt centre are in HP. K to row 72(78:80). Shape

shoulder using HP as follows: K 1 row Rt to Lt. Bring 2(2:3) Ns to HP at Rt edge of work. K 1 row to Rt and wrap outside N. K 1 row to Lt, bring 2(2:3) Ns at Rt edge to HP. Continue to do this, 2 Ns each time on small and medium sizes, 3 Ns then 2 twice on large size.

RC 82(88:90) take all shoulder Ns back to WP and K 1 row. Break MY, thread WY, K 6 rows and remove from machine. Repeat this shaping for Lt shoulder, reversing instructions as before.

Centre neck sts remain on machine. K 1 row T5 and cast off.

FIRST SHOULDER SEAM

With Rt side work facing you, replace sts Lt shoulder on machine. Take second garment piece, and with Rt sides tog replace sts

matching shoulder on Ns. K 1 row T5 and cast off.

NECK EDGE

This neck edge has been finished with several rows of crochet to give a slightly scalloped edge. Work as follows: with the Rt side of the fabric facing, work a row of dc along the edge to be trimmed, then work as follows: 1 dc into the 1st st, *3 ch, miss 1 st, 1 dc into next st, rep from * to end. Fasten off. Make second shoulder seam as first.

Armhole edge as for neck edge.

TO MAKE UP

Back st main seam from armhole to welt. Slip st welts. Sew in ends.

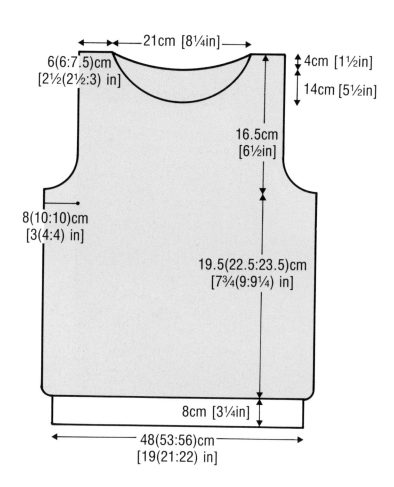

MOHAIR AND CHUNKY SILK JERSEY

TO FIT

Small: 82–87cm (32–34in)
across chest 51cm (20in)
finished length 56cm (22in)
sleeve length 43cm (17in)

Medium: 92–97cm (36–38in)
across chest 56cm (22in)
finished length 63cm (25in)
sleeve length 45cm (17¾in)

Large: 102–107cm (40–42in)
across chest 61cm (24in)
finished length 68cm (26¾in)
sleeve length 56cm (22in)

Extra large: 112–117cm (44-46in)
across chest 66cm (26in)
finished length 68cm (26¾in)
sleeve length 66cm (26in)

15cm (6in) allowance for ease

YARN

MY – 400g pink mohair,
Kaleidoscope collection (2115)
CY – 4×100g hanks spun silk 2/1s
metric in pale pink
　　J. Hyslop Bathgate & Co, Victoria
　　Works, Galashiels TD1 1NY.

TENSION

Measured over cables T8
Note: These cables are not latched up.
17 sts/16 rows = 10cm (4in)
　　Punch the card illustrated and cable over the 4 sts in silk. Cross sts 3 and 4 over 1 and 2 every 6 rows.

The N on either side of cable is out of work.

　　Please read pattern through carefully before starting to knit.

BACK

Using ribber cast on 86(96:104:110) sts in silk for 1:1 rib. T0/0 rib 30 rows. Transfer all sts to main bed. RC 000 insert punchcard. T8 K 2 rows mohair then start pattern, transferring sts at either side cabling sts to adjacent Ns. Silk in feeder 2 throughout. Extra-large size inc 1 st either end 2nd row.

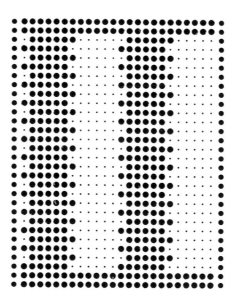

RC 26(38:44:44) cast off 6(7:8:9) sts at carr side. K 1 row then cast off 6(7:8:9) sts at carr side. K 1 row, dec 1 st at either end of row every

other row 3(3:4:4) times. Cont in pattern until RC 66(78:84:84). Set for Hold, carr at Rt. All Ns to Lt centre and 19(19:22:22) to Rt in HP. K 1 row, bring 1 N to HP. K 1 row and repeat until 22(22:25:25) Ns to Rt centre are in HP. RC 70(82:88:88). Break yarns, thread WY, K 6 rows and remove from machine.

　　Repeat this shaping, from RC 66(78:84:84), for Lt shoulder reversing instructions. Centre neck sts remain on machine. Pick up 1 st either side of these centre sts and K 6 rows T8 in silk. Cast off going behind sinker gates.

FRONT

As for back to row 54(66:72:72). Shape neck as follows using HP : carr at Rt, mark punchcard. All Ns to Lt centre in HP and 6(8:8:8) to Rt. K 1 row to Lt, bring 1 N to HP. K 1 row, etc and repeat until 22(22:25:25) Ns to Rt centre are in HP. K to row 70(82:88:88). Break yarns, thread WY, K 6 rows and remove from machine.

　　Repeat this shaping for Lt shoulder reading Lt for Rt and vice versa. Centre neck sts remain on machine. Pick up ¾ sts at either edge of neck shaping and replace on Ns. K 6 rows T8 silk then cast off, going behind sinker gates.

SHOULDER SEAMS

With Rt side garment facing you, replace sts Lt shoulder, front on Ns.

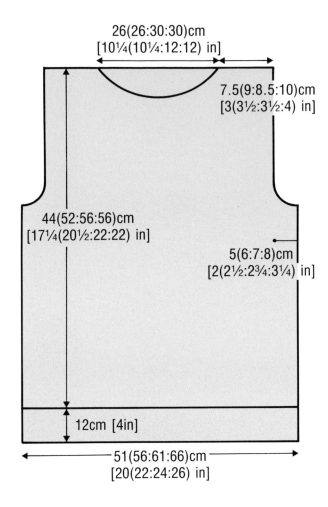

26(26:30:30)cm
[10¼(10¼:12:12) in]

7.5(9:8.5:10)cm
[3(3½:3½:4) in]

44(52:56:56)cm
[17¼(20½:22:22) in]

5(6:7:8)cm
[2(2½:2¾:3¼) in]

12cm [4in]

51(56:61:66)cm
[20(22:24:26) in]

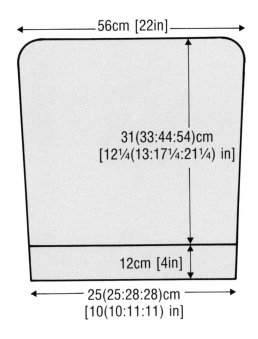

56cm [22in]

31(33:44:54)cm
[12¼(13:17¼:21¼) in]

12cm [4in]

25(25:28:28)cm
[10(10:11:11) in]

With Rt sides tog place sts Lt shoulder back, on same Ns. K 1 row mohair T8 and cast off loosely. Repeat for second shoulder.

SLEEVE

Using WY and every N cast on over 50 sts. RC 000 K 1 row T8 mohair. Set punchcard. K 1 row, start pattern, transferring sts beside 4 cable sts to adjacent Ns before knitting. K in cable pattern inc 1 st every row at carr side 44 times on small size. On medium size inc 1 st either end of row every 2 rows 12 times, then every 4 rows 15 times.

On large size inc 1 st every row 4 times then every 3 rows to 96 sts. On extra-large size inc 1 st every 3 rows to 96 sts. RC 44(48:68:92). Dec 1 st at either end row every other row 4(5:5:6) times. RC 52(58:78:104). Cast off loosely.

CUFF

Using ribber cast on 42(42:48:48) sts in silk for 1:1 rib. T0/0 rib 30 rows. Transfer all sts to main bed. Take sleeve and with Rt sides tog place sts on WY along bed beside sts of cuff. Pick up these sts and where necessary, place 2 sts on one N, evenly across the work. K 1 row T8 in silk and cast off loosely.

TO MAKE UP

With Rt sides tog place sleeve head along armhole edge and pin with pins at Rt angles to edge. Back st, using mohair. Back st main seam from cuff to welt. Slip st welts and cuffs with silk. Slip st collar edge. The collar is designed to roll outwards so that the garter st side is showing.

Cowl-neck jersey
Tie-design cardigan
Slash-neck jersey
Men's space-dyed waistcoat

WOOL

Cabled cricket jersey
Classic raglan-sleeved his and her jersey
Men's 'fisherman rib' jersey

COWL-NECK JERSEY

TO FIT

Small: 82–87cm (32–34in)
across chest 57cm (22½in)
finished length 57cm (22½in)
sleeve length, from dropped
shoulder 44cm (17½in)

Medium: 92–97cm (36–38in)
across chest 62cm (24½in)
finished length 64cm (25¼in)
sleeve length, from dropped
shoulder 48cm (19in)

Large: 102–107cm (40–42in)
across chest 67cm (26½in)
finished length 69cm (27¼in)
sleeve length, from dropped
shoulder 51cm (20in)

25cm (10in) allowance for ease.
1cm (0.4in) seam allowance.

YARN

1kg blue-grey merino/lambswool 4-
ply (colour number 20) (2 ends
yarn are used tog).
Designer Yarns, PO Box 18,
Longcroft, Keighley BD21 5AU.

TENSION

T6 stocking stitch
15.5 sts/21 rows = 10cm (4in)

Please read pattern through
carefully before starting to knit.

BACK

Using WY cast on 88(96:104) sts. K
6 rows. Thread MY. RC 000, K 22

rows T6. Place marker in contrast
yarn at Lt and Rt edges of work. K
to row 96(106:116). Set for Hold.
All Ns to Lt centre in HP and 17 to
Rt. K 1 row, bring 1 N to HP. K 1
row, bring 1 N to HP. Break MY,
thread WY, K 6 rows and remove
from machine.
　Repeat this shaping for Lt
shoulder, reading Rt for Lt and vice
versa. Centre neck sts remain on
machine. Thread WY, K 6 rows and
remove from machine.

FRONT

As for back to row 90(100:110).
Carr at Rt, set for Hold. All Ns to Lt
centre and 14 to Rt in HP. K 1 row,
bring 1 N to HP. K 1 row, bring 1 N
to HP, etc until 19 Ns to Rt centre
are in HP. K.
　Repeat shaping for Lt shoulder,
reading Lt for Rt and vice versa.
　Remove centre neck sts on 6
rows WY as before.

FIRST SHOULDER SEAM

With Rt side garment facing,
replace sts Lt shoulder on machine.
Pull out WY. Take 2nd garment
piece and replace sts on Ns in work,
matching shoulder and with Rt
sides tog. K 1 row T6 and cast off,
going behind sinker gates.

SLEEVE

Using closed-edge method, cast on
4 sts. Small: inc 1 st at Lt edge
every row. Medium: inc 1 st at Lt
edge every row. Large: inc 1 st

71

every row except 11, 22, 33, 44, 55 66th.

RC 46(57:66) K straight. RC 110(127:140) then dec 1 st every row at Lt edge of work on small and medium sizes. On large size dec 1 st every row except 11, 22, 33, 44, 55, 66th. Cast off remaining 4 sts.

Second sleeve K as 1st except that shaping takes place at Rt edge instead of Lt.

COWL NECK

With wrong side garment facing, pick up sts on WY along neck edge and replace on machine tog with ¾ those that remain along front neck edge. Thread MY, K 64 rows T6. Cast off going behind sinker gates.

Work second shoulder as first.

WELTS

Using ribber cast on 68(76:84) sts for 2:1 rib. Rib 28 rows T0/0. Rib 2 rows T4/4. Transfer all sts to main bed. Take back garment with wrong side facing, replace sts on WY on Ns in work, putting 2 sts on a N where necessary, evenly across the bed. K 1 row T6 and cast off loosely, going in front of sinker gates and using a claw weight hung just below st being cast off to stretch st. Repeat this for welt front of garment.

CUFFS

Using ribber cast on 40(50:52) sts for 2:1 rib. Rib 28 rows T0/0. Rib 2

rows T4/4. Transfer all sts to main bed. Take 1st sleeve and with wrong side facing pick up evenly along narrow edge. K 1 row T6 and cast off loosely as for welts. Repeat for second sleeve.

TO MAKE UP

With Rt sides tog match long edge sleeve to garment edge, marker at shoulder seam and underarm at marker on front and back. Pin. Back st. Back st main seam from cuff to welt on either side. Slip st cuffs, welts and cowl neck edge. The wrong side will become Rt side when cowl is rolled outwards. Sew in ends. Brush yarn lightly, if desired, with a teasel brush.

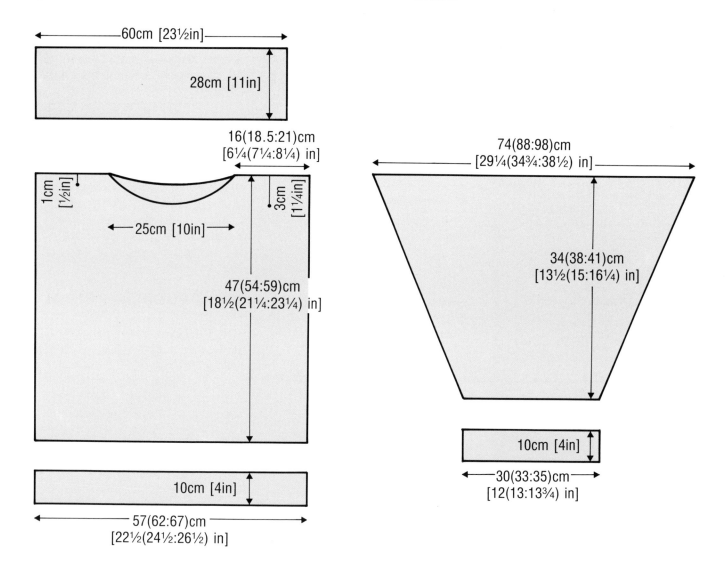

TIE-DESIGN CARDIGAN

TO FIT

Small: 82–87cm (32–34in)
across chest 51cm (20in)
finished length 56cm (22in)
sleeve length 43cm (17in)

Medium: 92–97cm (36–38in)
across chest 56cm (22in)
finished length 64cm (25¼in)
sleeve length 45cm (17¾in)

Large: 102–107cm (40–42in)
across chest 61cm (24in)
finished length 69cm (27¼in)
sleeve length 56cm (22in)

Extra-large: 112–117cm (44–46in)
across chest 66cm (26in)
finished length 74cm (29in)
sleeve length 64cm (25¼in)

YARN

Chunky New Zealand cross-bred
2/2.5s 100% wool
MY – 500(600:800:800)g T29
Balmoral navy
CY1 – 250g T25 raspberry + 2
skeins for large and extra-large
sizes
CY2 – 100g T12 old gold
J. Hyslop Bathgate & Co, Victoria
Works, Galashiels, Scotland
TD1 1NY.

Buttons: 7(8:8:9) plus 1 spare

TENSION

Measured over stocking st T5 : 14.5
sts/21 rows = 10cm (4in)

Please read pattern through
carefully before starting to knit.
This garment is knitted sideways
from cuff to cuff and the cuffs and
welts are added afterwards.

BACK

Using WY cast on over all Ns
22(22:30:30) sts and K 6 rows.
Break WY, thread MY. RC 000, K T5
22(26:36:42) rows. Change to CY1
and K 2 rows, CY2 K 2 rows, CY1 K
22 rows. Change to MY and inc 1 st
at Rt edge of work every 3 rows to
38(38:40:44) sts. RC 70(74:96:112)
using closed-edge method cast on
30(40:44:50) sts at Rt edge of work.
RC 80(90:112:132) make stripe as
before (26 rows) and at the same
time RC 103(113:135:150) dec 1 st
every row 4 times at Lt edge of
work, to shape back neck. RC
138(148:178:207) make stripe, this
time starting with 22 rows CY1, etc.
   RC 141(151:181:210) inc 1 st at
Lt edge of work every row 4 times
to complete neck shaping. RC
178(194:224:252) cast off
30(40:44:50) sts at Rt edge of work.
RC 200(216:258:296) dec 1 st at Rt
edge every 3 rows to 22(22:30:30)
sts. At the same time RC
200(204:258:296) make stripe
starting with 22 rows CY1 as before
(26 rows). RC 248(268:320:364)
break MY, thread WY, K 6 rows and
remove from machine.

FRONT

K 2 starting first piece well to the
Lt centre and second piece well to

Rt centre. K as for back to row
103(113:135:150). Shape front neck
dec 1 st at Lt/Rt edge of work every
row 14 times. RC 120(130:156:178)
break MY, thread WY, K 6 rows and
remove from machine.

WELTS

Back welt Using ribber cast on
74(81:88:96) sts CY1 for 2:1 rib. T3/
3 rib 2 rows, CY2 rib 2 rows, CY1 rib
2 rows, MY rib 20 rows. Transfer all
sts to main bed. Take back garment
and with Rt sides tog pick up sts
evenly along edge and place on Ns
in WP. K 1 row T5 and cast off.

Front welt K 2 alike. Using ribber
cast on 34(37:41:44) sts CY1 for 2:1
rib. T3/3 rib 2 rows, CY2 rib 2
rows, CY1 rib 2 rows, MY rib 20
rows.
   Transfer all sts to main bed and
attach front of garment as for back.

CUFFS

Join both shoulder seams first,
matching stripes, using back st.
   Using ribber cast on 40(40:50:50)
sts in CY1 for 2:1 rib. T3/3 rib 26
rows in stripe sequence as above,
then transfer all sts to main bed.
Take one sleeve and match
shoulder seam to centre ribbed
piece. Pick up sts on WY and
replace on Ns spacing extra sts out
evenly across the work. K 1 row T5
and cast off.
   Repeat for second cuff.

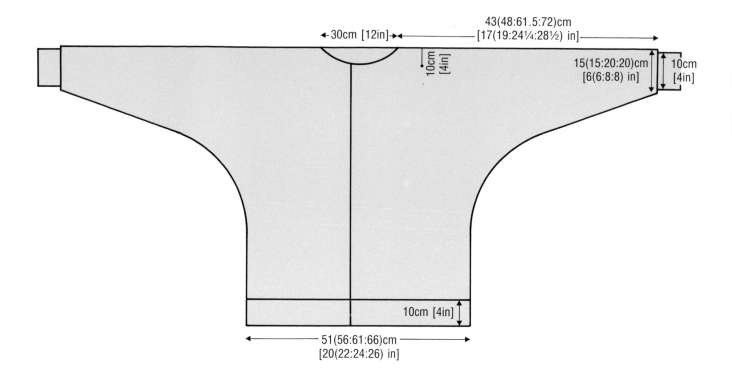

NECKBAND

Using ribber cast on 64(64:76:94) sts in CY1 for 2:1 rib. T3/3 rib 2 rows, CY2 rib 2 rows, CY1 rib 2 rows, MY rib 4 rows. Transfer all sts to main bed. Take main garment piece and lay neck edge along band Rt sides tog. Pick up sts and replace on Ns in WP. K 1 row T5 and cast off.

FRONT BANDS

Button band Using ribber cast on 72(82:88:98) sts in CY1 for 2:1 rib. T3/3 rib 2 rows, CY2 rib 2 rows, CY1 rib 2 rows, MY rib 6 rows.

Transfer all sts to main bed. K 1 row T5. Take Rt front and with Rt sides tog replace sts on WY on Ns in WP and those of welt. K 1 row T5 and cast off.

Buttonhole band Using ribber cast on 72(82:88:98) sts in CY1 for 2:1 rib. T3/3 rib 2 rows, CY2 rib 2 rows, CY1 rib 2 rows.

Change to MY and make buttonholes, transferring 1 st from bottom to top bed and 1 st from top to bottom bed using double-ended transfer tool. Make the 1st hole 4 Ns in from either end of band and the 2nd at the Rt 6 Ns in from the 1st hole. After that make the holes at 11 N intervals.

Attach band as for button band.

POCKETS

RC 000 using closed-edge method, cast on over all Ns 40 sts MY. K T5. RC 26 carr at Rt bring 20 sts at opposite side work to carr to HP. Using HP shape remaining 20 sts dec 1 st at both ends row every 2 rows 3 times. Cast off. Repeat this shaping for 20 sts still on machine.

Fold this piece in half and slip st edges tog, leaving 2 straight edges. When stitching underarm seam leave a gap above the welt the same width as the pocket opening. It is best to position the pocket by trying the garment on. When the main seam is complete, stitch ends of pocket to garment edge.

Second pocket as first.

TO MAKE UP

Back st underarm seam from cuff to welt. Slip st cuffs and welts. Weave ends of pattern colours back along line of colour on reverse of fabric. Sew on buttons.

SLASH-NECK JERSEY

TO FIT

Small: 82–87cm (32–34in)
across chest 53.5cm (21in)
finished length 64cm (25in)
sleeve length 44cm (17¼in)

Medium: 92–97cm (36–38in)
across chest 58.5cm (23in)
finished length 68.5cm (27in)
sleeve length 45cm (17¾in)

Large: 102–107cm (40–42in)
across chest 63.5cm (25in)
finished length 73.5cm (29in)
sleeve length 48cm (19in)

20cm (8in) allowance for ease

YARN

750(850g : 1kg) Chunky New
Zealand cross-bred 2/2.5s undyed
(T43)
J. Hyslop Bathgate & Co, Victoria
Works, Galashiels, Scotland
TD1 1NY.

TENSION

Measured over stocking st T5. Wash
swatch
14.5 sts/21 rows = 10cm (4in)

Please read pattern through
carefully before starting to knit.

BACK AND FRONT

Using ribber cast on 78(84:92) sts
for 2:1 rib T0/0 rib 9 rows. T5/5 rib
1 row. Transfer all sts to main bed.
  RC 000 carr at Rt, T5 K
84(94:98) rows. At carr side cast off
10 sts. K 1 row. At carr side cast off
10 sts. K 3(3:9) rows. Carr at Rt.
Follow instructions for yoke (p79)
Each set of 2 tucks counts as 4
rows. Re-set RC to agree with this.

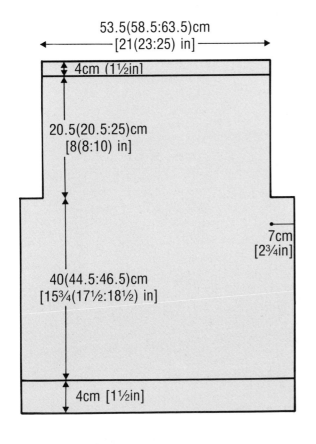

53.5(58.5:63.5)cm
[21(23:25) in]

4cm (1½in)

20.5(20.5:25)cm
[8(8:10) in]

7cm
[2¾in]

40(44.5:46.5)cm
[15¾(17½:18½) in]

4cm [1½in]

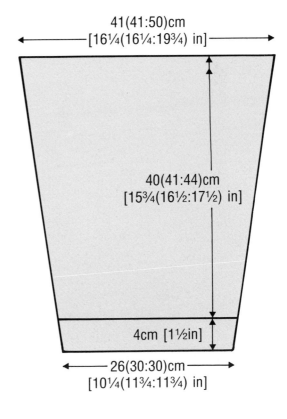

41(41:50)cm
[16¼(16¼:19¾) in]

40(41:44)cm
[15¾(16½:17½) in]

4cm [1½in]

26(30:30)cm
[10¼(11¾:11¾) in]

MANUAL TRANSFER PATTERN FOR YOKE AND CUFFS

K 4 rows T2, pick up 1st row loops
K 1 row T3
K 1 row T5
K4 rows T2, pick up 1st row of loops
K 1 row T3
K 2 rows T5, make 1st hole
K 2 rows T5, make 2nd hole, etc until 7 holes

K 3 rows T5
K 4 rows T2, pick up 1st row loops
K 1 row T3
K 1 row T5
K 4 rows T2, pick up 1st row loops
K 1 row T3

Make holes according to Fig 0, transferring all sts to Lt centre to Lt and all sts to Rt centre to Rt.

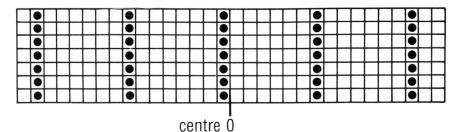

centre 0

□ : needle in work
◉ : lace

RC 118(128:138) K 1 row T5. Break MY, thread WY, K 6 rows and remove from machine.

SLEEVE

Using ribber cast on 38(44:44) sts for 2:1 rib. T0/0 rib 9 rows T5/5 rib 1 row. Transfer all sts to main bed. RC 000 as for yoke, make pattern over next 30 rows. Remember to re-set RC after each set of 2 tucks. RC 30 inc 1 st either end row every 3(4:4) rows to 72(72:78) sts. RC 88(90:102) break MY, thread WY, K 6 rows and remove from machine.

NECKBAND

K 2 alike. Using ribber cast on 58(64:72) sts T0/0. Rib 9 rows, T5/5 rib 1 row. Transfer all sts to main bed. K 1 row T5. Take main garment piece and with Rt sides tog, place sts on WY on those in

WP. K 1 row T5 and cast off loosely going in front of sinker gates and using a claw weight to stretch the st.

Repeat for second piece.

SHOULDER SEAM

Turn sleeve round so that Rt side is facing and replace sts on WY on machine. Take both main garment pieces and with Rt sides tog, pick up sts along edge of armhole evenly and place on sts in WP. K1 row T5 and cast off.

TO MAKE UP

Back st underarm where sleeve joins main garment piece. Back st main seam from cuff to welt, both sides. Slip st cuffs. Slip st extreme ends of neckband tog. It is a matter of individual preference how wide the neck opening should be.

MEN'S SPACE-DYED WAISTCOAT

TO FIT

Small: 92cm (36in)
across chest 49cm (19½in)
finished length 44cm (17¼in)
waist 73cm (29in)

Medium: 97cm (38in)
across chest 51cm (20in)
finished length 44cm (17¼in)
waist 84cm (33in)

Large: 102cm (40in)
across chest 53.75cm (21in)
finished length 44.5cm (17½in)
waist 88cm (34¾in)

Extra-large: 107cm (42in)
across chest 56.5cm (22in)
finished length 45cm (17¾in)
waist 92cm (36¼in)

5cm (2in) allowance made for fit
This pattern does not need a ribber

YARN

300g Colinette 'Island' wool, colour
    Merlin
    Colinette Yarns, Park Lane
    House, High Street, Welshpool,
    Powys, Wales.
Small amount black DK wool
Buttons: 4

TENSION

T6 stocking st
21 rows/15.5 sts = 10cm (4in)
Please read pattern through
carefully before starting to knit.

BACK

Using WY, cast on 62(65:68:72) sts.
Join in MY. RC 000 inc 1 st at either
end of row every 6(5:5:4) rows to
76(79:84:88) sts. K 0(5:0:4) rows.
RC 42(40:40:36). At carr side cast
off 5(5:5:6) sts. K 1 row. At carr
side cast off 5(5:5:6) sts. Dec 1 st
either end of row fully fashioned
(treble eyelet tool) every 9(10:8:9)
rows at 56(59:62:76) sts. K. RC
90(90:90:92). Set for Hold. Shape
shoulder as follows : at opposite
edge of work to carr bring 4(4:5:5)
Ns to HP. K 1 row. At opposite edge
of work to carr bring 3(4:5:5) Ns to
HP. K 1 row. Cont to shape Rt
shoulder in this way but also shape
back neck, as follows : at opposite
edge of work to carr bring all Ns to
HP plus 12(12:14:16) to Rt centre.
K 1 row. Bring 1 more N at centre
to HP. Bring 3(3:4:4) Ns at shoulder
edge to HP. K 1 row. Bring 1 N at
centre to HP. K 1 row and bring 1 N
at centre to HP. Bring last 3(3:4:4)
Ns at shoulder edge to HP.
Everything is now in HP.

Take back to C(D) position
13(14:14:14) Ns and K 1 row. Break
MY, thread WY and K 6 rows before
removing shoulder from machine.

Repeat shoulder and neck
shaping for Lt side, reversing
instructions and reading Lt for Rt.
This leaves centre neck sts on
machine.

Thread WY, K 6 rows and remove
from machine.

FRONT

K 2, reversing shapings for second
front.

Using the closed-edge method of
cast on, cast on 1 st all sizes. Wrap
and bring 2 more Ns to HP with the
carr set to K. K 1 row. Wrap and
bring 3 Ns to HP. K 1 row. Cont to
inc by 3 sts every row until there
are 30 sts, small and medium sizes;
32 sts, large size; and 33, extra-
large size. RC 10(10:12:12).

RC 000 K to RC 42(40:40:36)
keeping Rt edge straight and inc as
follows at Lt edge : inc 1 st every
6(5:5:4) rows to 36(38:40:42) sts.
At Lt edge cast off 5(5:5:6) sts. K 1
row. At Lt edge cont to dec 1 st
fully fashioned every 9(10:8:9) rows
to row 90(90:90:92) and at the
same time at Rt edge dec 1 st fully
fashioned every 4(4:3:3) rows until
13(14:14:14) sts remain. At row
90(90:90:92) with carr at Rt and set
for Hold, bring 3(4:5:5) Ns to HP at
armhole edge. K 1 row to Lt and
cont shaping at neck edge at the
same time. Shape shoulder as for
back : bringing Ns to HP when carr
is at opposite side of work in this
order : small 4:3:3:3; medium
4:4:3:3; large 5:5:4:4; extra-large
5:5:4:4 Ns. When shaping is
complete bring all shoulder Ns to
WP and K 1 row across on main
tension. Break yarn, thread WY and
K 6 rows before removing from
machine.

SHOULDER SEAMS

Replace sts of Lt shoulder back on machine with Rt side garment facing. Take front of garment with Rt side facing machine, place sts Lt shoulder on those of Lt back. K 1 row T6 and cast off going behind sinker gates. Repeat this for second shoulder.

ARMHOLE BANDS

With wrong side of work facing you, pick up sts around armhole evenly, leaving every 4th st. Thread up MY, K 3 rows T2. Take out MY and thread black. K 1 row black T2. K 1 row T10, K 1 row T2. Break black and thread MY. K3 rows. Break MY, thread WY, K 6 rows and remove from machine.

Repeat for second armhole.
Back st side seams.

FRONT BANDS

With wrong side of work facing you, pick up sts along edge of garment, starting from shoulder seam and ending at point of front shaping. The opposite band will go from shoulder seam and down front to point of V and the back neck will be knitted separately. The Lt front band needs buttonholes at 10 st intervals, 4 in all. (See method for buttonholes in stocking st band, page 00.) The fourth piece will go across back waist to point of shaping, to match front. Pick up sts in same ratio as before. Thread MY, K 3 rows T2. Take out MY, thread black and K 1 row T2, 1 row T10 and 1 row T2. Break black and thread MY. K 3 rows. Remove from machine on 6 rows of WY.

This is the basic method. At the end of the band that meets the point of the front (marked A on Fig 0) this band must be mitred. At this end only inc 1 st every row to fold line (row 5), then dec 1 st every row to finish.

TO MAKE UP

Slip st mitres in MY. Slip st bands to main garment. Back st side seams, if you've not already done so.

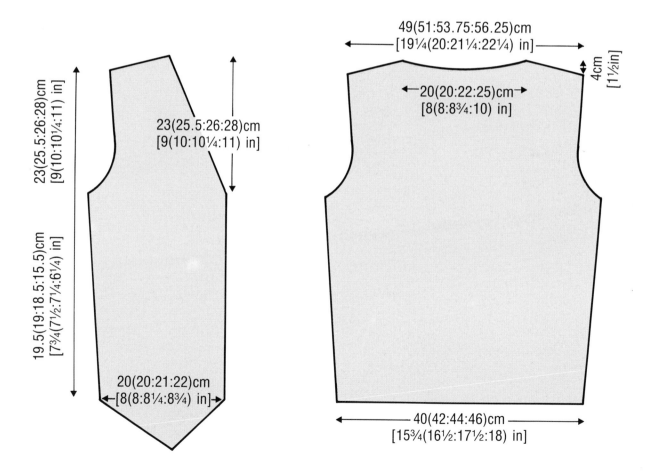

23(25.5:26:28)cm
[9(10:10¼:11) in]

19.5(19:18.5:15.5)cm
[7¾(7½:7¼:6¼) in]

20(20:21:22)cm
[8(8:8¼:8¾) in]

49(51:53.75:56.25)cm
[19¼(20:21¼:22¼) in]

4cm
[1½in]

20(20:22:25)cm
[8(8:8¾:10) in]

40(42:44:46)cm
[15¾(16½:17½:18) in]

CABLED CRICKET JERSEY

TO FIT

Small: 92–97cm (36–38in)
across chest 56cm (22in)
finished length 62.5cm (24½in)
sleeve length, overarm 57cm
(22½in)

Medium: 97–102cm (38–40in)
across chest 58.5cm (23in)
finished length 64cm (25¼in)
sleeve length, overarm 57.5cm
(22½in)

Large: 107–112cm (42–44in)
across chest 63.5cm (25in)
finished length 65cm (25½in)
sleeve length, overarm 58cm (23in)

YARN

1kg chunky Aran in cream
    Nethy Products, Kirkshaws Road,
    Coatbridge, Scotland ML5 4SL.

TENSION

Measured over cable pattern
T7 stocking st 15 sts/22 rows =
10cm (4in)
Each cable measures 2cm across,
equivalent to 3 sts.

CABLE

Worked over 4 sts with 1 N either
side of cable in NWP and 6(6:8) Ns
in WP before next cable. When
arranging Ns before knitting, work
outwards from centre of machine.

   Twist cables as follows : twist sts
1 and 2 under 3 and 4. K 6 rows.

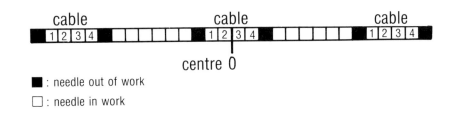

: needle out of work
: needle in work

Twist 3 and 4 under 1 and 2. K 6
rows. Before knitting 6th row each
time, bring Ns from NWP to WP
and then K. Return empty Ns to
NWP. This creates extra yarn for
twisting the cable. The ladder
formed by the empty N in each
case is latched up using the latch
tool on the back of the work, when
the last row of the garment piece is
reached.

BACK

Using ribber cast on 88(91:99) sts
for 2:1 rib. Rib 21(23:23) rows T0/0,
1 row T6/6. Transfer all sts to main
bed. K 1 row T7. Break MY, thread
WY, K 6 rows and remove from
machine. Replace work on machine,
but this time over 106(109:114) Ns
with the extra sts evenly spaced.
Pick up a loop from an adjacent st
on the row below, and place it on
the empty N in each case. Arrange
N bed as chart, starting from centre
and working outwards. RC 000 T7
K to row 77(70:74) maintaining
cable pattern throughout.
   At carr side cast off 6(7:8) sts. K
1 row. At carr side cast off 6(7:8)
sts, then cast off 1 st at either side
of work every other row, 4 times.
Then cast off 1 st either side of

work every 4th row 2(3:3) times
(total 12(14:15) sts dec each
side). Cont in cable pattern to row
119(119:129). Shape shoulder as
follows : at opposite side of work to
carr, take 4(4:5) Ns back to NWP
using nylon cord. Do this at each
edge of the work. Cont to dec at
both sides as follows : small and
medium sizes, 4:4:4:5 sts, large size,
5:5:5:6 sts.
   RC 124(128:137), start neck
shaping. A third piece of nylon cord
must be used here. All Ns to Lt of
centre on nylon cord and 15 to Rt.
Take a further N back to NWP on
nylon cord every row at neck edge
until 18 are in HP, at the same time
cont shoulder shaping.
   RC 128(132:141) all Ns in NWP.
Put all shoulder sts back into WP, K
1 row T7. Latch up cables. Break
MY, thread WY, K 6 rows and
remove shoulder from machine.
Repeat shoulder and neck shaping
for Lt side of work keeping cables
going throughout. Remove centre
neck sts on 6 rows WY.

FRONT

As for back to row 72(68:84).
   Take all sts to Lt centre back to
NWP using nylon cord. Carr at Rt.

Cont to cable and shape V-neck as follows : Lt edge of work dec 1 st fully fashioned (treble eyelet tool) every 3rd row. 17(17:21) sts. K. At the same time, Rt edge of work on small size, cast off 6 sts RC 72 then 1 st every other row 4 times and 1 st every 4th row twice.

On medium size RC 70 Rt edge of work cast off 7 sts. K 1 row, cast off 7 sts, then 1 st every other row 4 times, followed by 1 st every 4th row three times. On large size RC 74 cast off 8 sts Rt edge work. K 1 row, cast off 8 sts, then 1 st every other row 4 times followed by 1 st every 4th row three times.

RC 119(119:129) start shoulder shaping. Carr at Lt take back 4(4:5) sts at Rt on nylon cord. Then 4(4:5), 4(4:5) and 5(5:6) sts. RC 128(132:141) all sts on nylon cord,

bring back to WP and K 1 row T7. Latch up cables. Break MY, thread WY, K 6 rows and remove from machine.

Repeat neck and shoulder shapings for Lt side of work, reversing instructions reading Lt for Rt.

FIRST SHOULDER SEAM

Rt side of garment facing, replace sts Rt shoulder back of garment, on machine. Pull out WY. Take front of garment and, with Rt sides tog, replace sts Rt shoulder on those already on machine. K 1 row T7 and cast off going behind sinker gates.

Second shoulder seam is knitted as first when neckband is complete.

NECKBAND

Using ribber cast on 77(80:83) sts for 2:1 rib. Rib 9 rows T0/0 1 row T6/6. Transfer all sts to main bed. This band goes across the back neck and down Rt front edge to point of V. Take main garment pieces and replace back neck sts on those of band, then pick up evenly along front edge. K 1 row across these sts T7 and cast off very loosely, going in front of sinker gates and using a claw weight to stretch the st.

Using ribber cast on 41(44:47) sts for 2:1 rib. Rib 9 rows T0/0, 1 row T6/6. Transfer all sts to main bed. This band goes down Lt edge of V to the point, so there will be a seam on the shoulder joining the 2 pieces of neckband. Take main

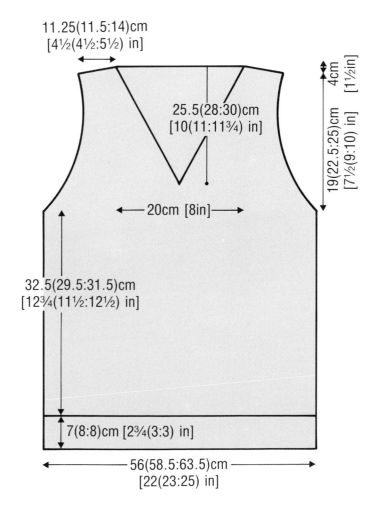

11.25(11.5:14)cm
[4½(4½:5½) in]

25.5(28:30)cm
[10(11:11¾) in]

4cm [1½in]

19(22.5:25)cm
[7½(9:10) in]

20cm [8in]

32.5(29.5:31.5)cm
[12¾(11½:12½) in]

7(8:8)cm [2¾(3:3) in]

56(58.5:63.5)cm
[22(23:25) in]

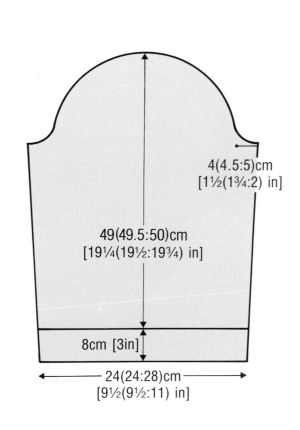

4(4.5:5)cm
[1½(1¾:2) in]

49(49.5:50)cm
[19¼(19½:19¾) in]

8cm [3in]

24(24:28)cm
[9½(9½:11) in]

garment pieces and pick up sts evenly down Lt front edge. K 1 row T7 and cast off loosely as before.

SLEEVE

Using ribber cast on 36(36:42) sts for 2:1 rib. Rib 23 rows T0/0, 1 row T6/6. Transfer all sts to main bed. K 1 row T7. Break MY, thread WY, K 6 rows and remove from machine. Replace this on machine over 42(43:49) Ns evenly. Pick up a loop from an adjacent st on the row below an empty N. Starting from centre arrange the Ns according to chart with 1st cable at centre. The number of cables will inc as work progresses. Start cable as soon as sufficient sts are present.

Inc 1 st either end of row every 7(6:6) rows to 70(82:88) sts. K to row 128(134:134). Carr side cast off 6(7:8) sts. K 1 row cast off 6(7:8) sts. Then cast off 5 sts at either side of work and 1 st either side of work every 4th row 3(3:4) times. Total number of sts dec either side 14(14:17). Then dec 1 st either end of row every other row 11(17:17) times. K to row 110(110:120) and latch up cables. Cast off.

TO MAKE UP

Join second shoulder seam as first. Back st sleeve underarm seam and side seams main garment. Slip st welts and cuffs. Turn main garment inside out and place sleeve head in armhole. Pin. Back st firmly. Slip st neckband at point of V.

CLASSIC RAGLAN-SLEEVED HIS AND HER JERSEY

TO FIT

Small: 82–87cm (32–34in)
across chest 53.5cm (21in)
finished length 56cm (22in)
sleeve length underarm 46cm (18in)

Medium: 92–97cm (36–38in)
across chest 58.5cm (23in)
finished length 64cm (25¼in)
sleeve length underarm 49cm (19¼in)

Large: 102–107cm (40–42in)
across chest 63.5cm (25in)
finished length 69cm (27¼in)
sleeve length underarm 66cm (26in)

Extra-large: 112–117cm (44–46in)
across chest 68.5cm (27in)
finished length 74cm (29in)
sleeve length underarm 69cm (27¼in)

20cm (8in) allowance for ease

YARN

2(2:3:3) cones Designer tweed (97% wool, 3% cotton) in black or navy
A. C. Wood (speciality fibres) Ltd, Mohair Mills, Gibson Street, Bradford BD3 9TS.

TENSION

T6 stocking st
16.5 sts/19.5 rows = 10cm (4in)

BACK

Using ribber cast on 88(96:104:113) sts for 2:1 rib. T0/0 rib 28 rows. T5/5 rib 2 rows. Transfer all sts to main bed. RC 000. T6 K 58(72:76:80) rows. Carr at Rt, cast off 5(8:8:10) sts at carr side. K 1 row. Cast off 5(8:8:10) sts at carr side. Then, small size : dec 1 st either end of row, every 2 rows 24 times and 1 st every row twice, using three-pronged tool (fully fashioned); medium size : dec 1 st fully fashioned either end of row every 2 rows 25 times; large size : dec 1 st fully fashioned either end of row every 2 rows 29 times; extra-large size : dec 1 st fully fashioned either end of row every 2 rows 29 times. RC 109(125:136:144). Break MY, thread WY, K 6 rows and remove from machine.

CLASSIC RAGLAN-SLEEVED HIS AND HER JERSEY

FRONT

As for back to row 96(112:120:130). Continue to dec as for back and at the same time set for HP. All Ns to Lt centre and 6(8:8:8) to Rt in HP. K 1 row. Bring 1 more N to HP, K 1 row, bring 1 N to HP, etc until 13(15:15:15) Ns to Rt centre are in HP. RC 109(125:136:144). No sts remain.

SLEEVE

K 2 alike. Using ribber cast on 50(54:54:58) sts for 2:1 rib. T0/0 rib 28 rows. T5/5 rib 2 rows. Transfer all sts to main bed. RC 000 K inc 1 st either end of row every 7(9:9:8) rows. 70(74:82:88) sts. K to row 74(96:128:134). Carr at Rt cast off 5(8:8:10) sts. K 1 row. Cast off 5(8:8:10) sts, then dec 1 st fully fashioned either end of row,

small size: every 2 rows 25 times;

medium size: every 2 rows 26 times;

large size: every 2 rows 29 times;

extra-large size: every 2 rows 31 times.

8sts remain. Break MY, thread WY, K 6 rows and remove knitting from machine.

NECKBAND

Mattress st 3 shoulder seams. Using ribber cast on 74(80:82:86) sts. T0/0 rib 10 rows. T5/5 rib 1 row. Transfer all sts to main bed. Pick up all sts on WY and replace on machine. K 1 row T6. Cast off loosely, going in front of sinker gates.

TO MAKE UP

Mattress st 4th shoulder. Back st main seam from wrist to waist. Slip st cuffs and welts. Sew in ends. Wash by hand in lukewarm water. Spin and lay flat to dry. Steam press.

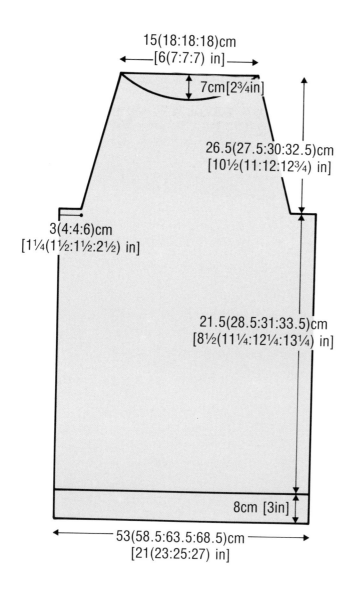

15(18:18:18)cm
[6(7:7:7) in]

7cm[2¾in]

26.5(27.5:30:32.5)cm
[10½(11:12:12¾) in]

3(4:4:6)cm
[1¼(1½:1½:2½) in]

21.5(28.5:31:33.5)cm
[8½(11¼:12¼:13¼) in]

8cm [3in]

53(58.5:63.5:68.5)cm
[21(23:25:27) in]

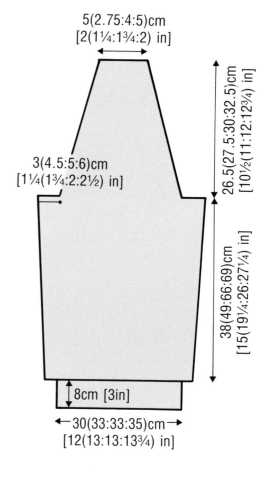

5(2.75:4:5)cm
[2(1¼:1¾:2) in]

26.5(27.5:30:32.5)cm
[10½(11:12:12¾) in]

3(4.5:5:6)cm
[1¼(1¾:2:2½) in]

38(49:66:69)cm
[15(19¼:26:27¼) in]

8cm [3in]

30(33:33:35)cm
[12(13:13:13¾) in]

MEN'S 'FISHERMAN RIB' JERSEY

TO FIT

Small: 87–92cm (34–36in)
across chest 51.5cm (20¼in)
finished length 63.5cm (25in)
sleeve length 56cm (22in)

Medium: 97–102cm (38–40in)
across chest 56cm (22in)
finished length 66cm (26in)
sleeve length 56cm (22in)

Large: 107–112cm (42–44in)
across chest 62cm (24½in)
finished length 69cm (27¼in)
sleeve length 66cm (26in)

Extra-large: 112–117cm (44–46in)
across chest 63.5cm (25in)
finished length 74cm (29in)
sleeve length 69cm (27¼in)

10cm (4in) allowance for ease +
1cm (0.4in) seam allowance

YARN

2(2:2:3) cones Brora Soft Spun
  BSS28
  T. M. Hunter Ltd, Sutherland
  Wool Mills, Brora, Scotland
  KW9 6NA.

TENSION

Measured over tuck st (Knitmaster
card 1, Jones/Brother card 1p), T4.
Swatch washed according to
Hunter's recommendations before
measuring

Pages 90–1: (main picture) *Men's
'fisherman rib' jersey;* (inset) *Classic
raglan-sleeved his and her jersey*

Please read pattern through
carefully before starting to knit.
This yarn makes a very good mock
rib. There is no neck shaping as
such. The neck is cut out when the
garment pieces are complete. A
separate neckband is knitted and
stitched on by hand. This is known
as 'cut and sew'.

BACK AND FRONT

Using ribber cast on 74(80:88:90)
sts in MY for 2:1 rib. T0/0 rib 25
rows, T4/4 rib 1 row. Break MY,
thread WY, K 6 rows and remove
from machine. Replace these sts on
64(70:78:80) Ns with 2 sts on 1 N at
even intervals across the bed.
  RC 000 carr at Rt K 1 row T4. Set
punchcard and K in tuck st to RC
114(114:116:134). Carr at Rt cast
off 5(5:7:7) sts at carr side. K 1 row
cast off 5(5:7:7) sts at carr side. K 1
row then dec 1 st at carr side and
repeat twice. 7(7:9:9) sts dec in all
at each edge of work. Cont in tuck
st to RC 198(210:222:240). Change
to stocking st, K 1 row T4. Break
MY, thread WY, K 6 rows and
remove from machine. K2.

SHOULDER SEAM

Take back garment and replace sts
on WY on machine, Rt side facing.
Take front garment and place sts
on WY on Ns in work, Rt sides tog.
K 1 row T6 and cast off loosely
going in front of sinker gates and
using claw weight to stretch sts.

SLEEVE

K 2 alike. Using ribber cast on 34(36:42:44) sts in MY for 2:1 rib. T0/0 rib 25 rows, T4/4 rib 1 row. Transfer sts to main bed. Break MY, thread WY, K 6 rows and remove from machine. Replace these sts on 30(30:36:36) Ns, spacing out the extra sts evenly across the work. Pull out WY.

RC 000 carr at Rt, K 1 row T4. Set punchcard and K in tuck st inc 1 st at either end of row every 11(8:10:11) rows to 56(64:70:70) sts. Cont in tuck st to row 150(150:182:192). Carr at Rt dec 1 st at either end of row every 3rd row 7(7:9:9) times. 42(50:52:52) sts remain. RC 172(172:210:220). Cast off loosely.

NECKBAND

Using ribber cast on 88 sts for 2:1 rib. T0/0 rib 10 rows. Bring up all empty Ns for full N rib and K 1 row T2/2. Set for circular knitting T5/5 and K 3(3:4:4) rows on each bed. Break MY, thread WY, K 6 rows on each bed and remove from machine.

CUT AND SEW NECK

See page 123.

TO MAKE UP

Attach band by back st through row of loops next to WY on outside of work, then slip st through loops on inside of garment. Pull out WY.

Back st main seam from cuff to welt each side (wrong side of work is Rt side of garment). Slip st cuffs and welts. Wash finished garment according to yarn manufacturer's recommendations.

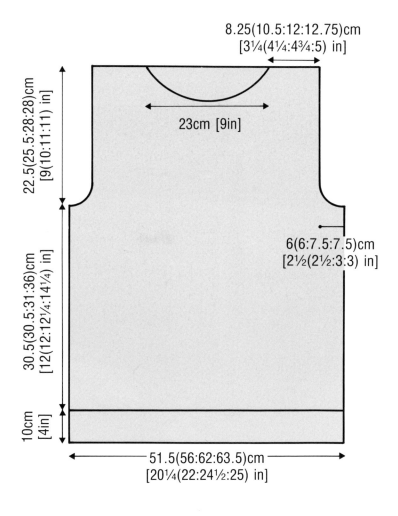

8.25(10.5:12:12.75)cm
[3¼(4¼:4¾:5) in]

23cm [9in]

22.5(25.5:28:28)cm
[9(10:11:11) in]

6(6:7.5:7.5)cm
[2½(2½:3:3) in]

30.5(30.5:31:36)cm
[12(12:12¼:14¼) in]

10cm
[4in]

51.5(56:62:63.5)cm
[20¼(22:24½:25) in]

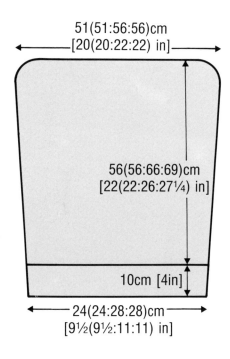

51(51:56:56)cm
[20(20:22:22) in]

56(56:66:69)cm
[22(22:26:27¼) in]

10cm [4in]

24(24:28:28)cm
[9½(9½:11:11) in]

4-ply all-over patterned jersey
Full-length coat

MOHAIR

Raglan-sleeved cardigan
Lacy sweater in mixed yarns

4-PLY ALL-OVER PATTERNED JERSEY

TO FIT

Small: 81–87cm (32–34in)
across chest 57cm (22½in)
finished length 50cm (20in)
sleeve length 39cm (15½in)

Medium: 92–102cm (36–40in)
across chest 62cm (24½in)
finished length 53cm (21in)
sleeve length 40cm (15¾in)

These measurements are approximate. This is a short style fitting onto the waist

YARN

MY – 350g cone charcoal 4-ply mohair Fine Art (77% mohair 23% polyester)
CY – 350g cone white 4-ply mohair Fine Art
A. C. Wood (speciality fibres) Ltd, Mohair Mills, Gibson Street, Bradford BD3 9TS

TENSION

T1 chunky machine measured over Fair Isle
T6 standard gauge machine ribs only
18 sts/25 rows = 10cm (4in)

Note: This pattern makes use of both the chunky machine and the standard gauge machine with ribber. The gathered waist is achieved by knitting the welts on the ribber of the standard gauge machine, after the main garment pieces have been knitted on the chunky machine.

To prepare the mohair for knitting, spray cone of yarn thoroughly with silicone spray and place in a sealed plastic bag. Leave this overnight before using. *Do not spray machine with silicone.*

Always use the close knit bar on the chunky machine when knitting with mohair, whether it is 4-ply mohair or chunky. This will give a firmer rib and make knitting easier.

Please read pattern through carefully before starting to knit.

BACK

Cast on using WY on chunky machine, 105(114) sts. K in Fair Isle T1 to row 108(114). Shape neck as follows : set carr for Hold.

Bring all Ns to Lt of centre to HP and 14(16) to Rt. Mark punchcard. K 1 row to Lt. Bring 1 N to HP. K 1 row to Rt. Bring 1 N to HP, etc until 19(21) Ns to Rt of centre are in HP. Continue knitting in Fair Isle to row 118(124). Break yarn. Thread WY, K 6 rows and remove shoulder from machine.

Carr at Rt. All Ns except 14(16) to Lt centre in WP. Reset punchcard to row marked. Thread up both colours and K Lt shoulder to match Rt, reversing shapings.

Centre neck sts remain on machine. Pick up every loop and every other knot along neck edge beside neck sts already on machine and K 1 row across these sts on T1. Transfer every other st to adjacent N. K 10 rows T0. K 1 row T10. K 9 rows T0 and 1 row T1. Break MY, thread WY, K 6 rows and remove garment from machine.

FRONT

As for back to row 94(100). Mark punchcard. Shape neck as follows : all Ns to Lt centre and 6(8) to Rt in

HP. K 1 row to Lt. Bring 2 Ns to HP and wrap outside N. K 1 row to Rt. Bring 2 Ns to HP. K 1 row to Lt. Bring 1 N to HP. Continue to bring 1 N to HP on each row until 19(21) Ns to Rt of centre are in HP. K to row 118(124) in Fair Isle. Break MY, thread WY, K 6 rows and remove from machine. Repeat shaping for Lt shoulder, reversing instructions. Centre neck sts remain on machine. Pick up every loop and every other knot along neck edge beside neck sts on machine and K 1 row across these sts T1. Transfer every other st to adjacent N. K 10 rows T0. K 1 row T10. K 9 rows T0 and last row T1. Break MY and thread WY. K 6 rows and remove garment from machine.

SLEEVE

K 2 alike. Cast on using WY 48(52) sts. T1 K in Fair Isle to row 86(90). At the same time inc 1 st at carr side every row to 100(110) sts. At

row 86(90), cast off loosely using a claw weight to stretch the sts, and going in front of the sinker gates.

WELTS

Using the standard gauge machine and ribber, cast on 130(138) sts in MY for 1:1 rib. Rib 30(38) rows T6. Transfer all sts to main bed. Take back/front of garment and with Rt side facing rib, replace sts on WY on Ns in use. There will be an empty st every 5th(4th) N because there are more sts in the rib than the body pieces.

Cast off loosely using a claw weight to keep the sts loose and going in front of the sinker gates.

CUFFS

76(80) sts and 30(38) rows. As welts.

SHOULDER SEAM

Replace sts Lt shoulder, front of

garment on chunky machine. With Rt sides tog, match Lt shoulder back garment to these and replace sts on same Ns. K 1 row MY T1 and cast off loosely as before. Both shoulder seams are the same.

NECKBAND

When shoulder seams are complete, slip st first row of loops (those next to WY) to neck edge sts, being careful to match the lines of rib. This gives a fairly elastic finish.

TO MAKE UP

Back st head of sleeve to main garment piece, making sure that centre sleeve is at shoulder seam and underarms match. Back st main seam from wrist to waist. Slip st welts and cuffs and neckband seam. Sew in ends by weaving back along row same colour or weaving into seam edge.

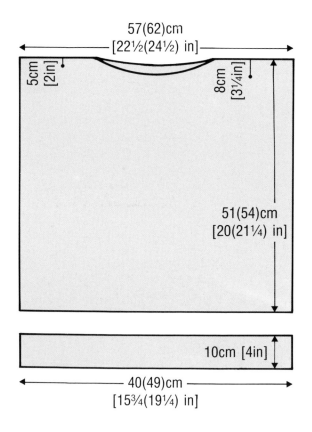

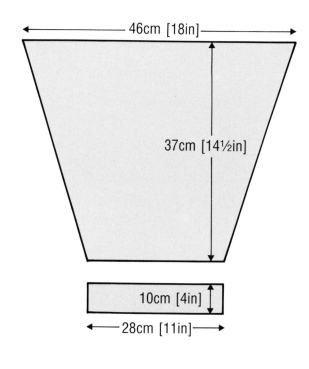

FULL-LENGTH COAT

TO FIT

Small: 82–87cm (32–34in)
across chest 51cm (20in)
finished length (mid-calf) 112cm
(44in)
sleeve underarm 46cm (18in)

Medium: 92–97cm (36–38in)
across chest 54cm (21¼in)
finished length (mid-calf) 112cm
(44in)
sleeve underarm 48cm (19in)

Large: 102–107cm (40–42in)
across chest 61cm (24in)
finished length (mid-calf) 117cm
(46in)
sleeve underarm 48cm (19in)

**Extra-large: 112–117cm (44–
46in)**
across chest 66cm (26in)
finished length (mid-calf) 117cm
(46in)
sleeve underarm 51cm (20in)

YARN

This stunning coat works well in a
variety of colourways, details of
which are given below.
　See the photographs on pages
98–9 and 102–3 for colour
illustrations of the alternatives.

2 cones Gold Award Mohair
　A. C. Wood (speciality fibres)
　Ltd, Mohair Mills, Gibson Street,
　Bradford BD3 9TS

4(4:5:5) skeins One-Zero 100%
　wool
　Colinette Yarns, Park Lane
　House, High Street, Welshpool,
　Powys, Wales

4 colourways:

MY – Kaleidoscope mohair 2917
　　green with One-Zero no 33 (CY)
MY – Kaleidoscope mohair 2378 red
　　with One-Zero no 14 (CY)
MY – Cocktail range mohair 3408
　　purple with One-Zero no 43 (CY)
MY – Cocktail range mohair 3407
　　dark blue with One-Zero no 57
　　(CY)

1 cone Supersheen in main colour
　Yeoman Yarns Ltd, 31 High
　Street, Kibworth, Leicester
　LE8 0HS.

Buttons: 8 plus 1 spare

Note: Thread the Supersheen up
with MY mohair and run as one
yarn. This supports the mohair and
helps prevent the possibility of
'give' in the finished garment, while
also adding body. It does not show.

TENSION

T9 for Fair Isle throughout

Punchcard 1: 14 sts/17 rows =
10cm (4in)
Punchcard 2: 16 sts/18 rows =
10cm (4in)

BACK

Using ribber cast on
96(106:114:114) sts in MY for 1:1
rib. Rib 6 rows T5/5. Transfer all sts
to main bed.
　RC 000 insert punchcard 1,
mohair in feeder 1 (A), One-Zero in
feeder 2 (B) throughout.
　T9, K in Fair Isle dec 1 st either
end row every 15(17:18:18) rows.
RC 112(106:108:108) start
punchcard 2.
　K in Fair Isle to row
140(138:144:144). Carr at Rt cast
off 5(6:8:7) sts. K 1 row cast off
5(6:8:7) sts. K in Fair Isle dec 1 st
either end row every 2 rows (small

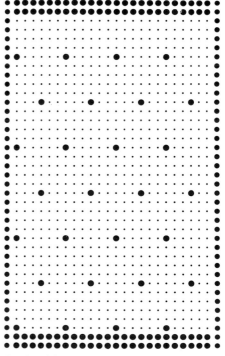

Punchcard 1

97

and medium), 1 st either end row every 2 rows (large) 1 st either end row every 2 rows × 29, then 1 st every row × 10 (extra-large). 20(28:31:32) sts remain.

RC 188(188:196:196) break MY and CY. Thread WY, K 6 rows and remove from machine.

FRONT

Using ribber cast on 50(52:56:60) sts in MY for 1:1 rib. T5/5, rib 6 rows. Transfer all sts to main bed.

RC 000 insert punchcard 1. T9, K in Fair Isle dec 1 st at Rt every 15(17:18:18) rows. RC 112(106:108:108) start punchcard 2. K in Fair Isle to row 140(138:144:144).

Carr at Rt cast off 5(6:8:7) sts. K 1 row. Cont in Fair Isle dec 1 st at Rt every 2 rows (small size × 21 and medium size × 24), dec 1 st every 2 rows × 23, then every row × 4 (large), dec 1 st every 2 rows × 25 (extra-large).

RC 166(166:174:180) carr at Rt, using nylon cord, take back to NWP 6(6:7:8) sts at Lt edge of work. K 1 row, 2 sts to NWP at Lt. K 1 row, 2 sts to NWP at Lt. K 1 row, 1 st to NWP. Cont to take 1 st to NWP at Lt on nylon cord each row until 14(14,17,19) sts at Lt are in NWP. K to row 188(188:196:196) remembering to cont to dec at Rt throughout. Remove sts on nylon cord by K 6 rows WY.

Knit second front as for first, reversing shapings, ie reading Rt for Lt and vice versa.

SLEEVE

Using WY cast on over every N 44(48:54:62) sts.

Insert punchcard 1. RC 000 T9, K in Fair Isle to RC 009 then inc 1 st either end row every 5 rows (66 sts), (small). Inc 1 st either end row every 6 rows (70 sts), (medium). K 4 rows then inc 1 st either end row every 8 rows (78 sts), (large). K in Fair Isle inc 1 st either end row

every 6 rows (86 sts), (extra-large).

Note that punchcard 2 must be inserted on row 36(34:36:40).

RC 64(66:68:72) carr at Rt cast off 5(6:8:7) sts, K 1 row. Cast off 5(6:8:7) sts.

RC 66(68:70:74) dec 1 st either end row every 2 rows (small and medium). Dec 1 st either end row every 2 rows × 26, then every row × 2 (large). Dec 1 st either end row every 2 rows × 25, then every row × 6 (extra-large). 8(10:10:13) sts remain.

Break MY and CY. Thread up WY, K 6 rows and remove from machine.

CUFFS

Using ribber, cast on 34(36:40:40) sts in MY for 1:1 rib. Rib 26 rows T0/0. Transfer all sts to main bed. Rt sides tog, pick up sts on WY 1st

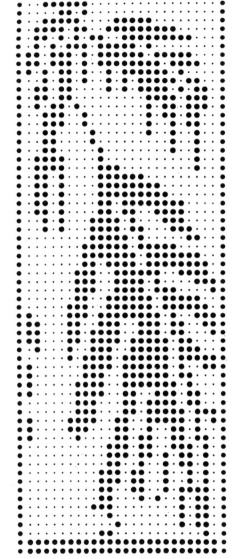

Punchcard 2

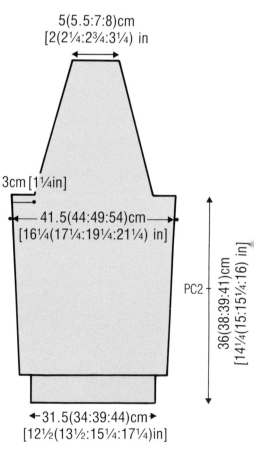

5(5.5:7:8)cm
[2(2¼:2¾:3¼) in]

3cm [1¼in]

41.5(44:49:54)cm
[16¼(17¼:19¼:21¼) in]

PC2

36(38:39:41)cm
[14¼(15:15¼:16) in]

31.5(34:39:44)cm
[12½(13½:15¼:17¼)in]

sleeve and replace on machine with 2 sts on each N where appropriate. K 1 row T9 then cast off loosely.

FRONT BANDS

Using ribber, cast on for 1:1 rib 15 sts in MY. Rib 260(260:274:274) rows T0/0. Check for length.

Button band as above, making buttonholes at rows 4, 22, 40, 58, 76, 94, 112 etc by transferring 1 st from top bed to bottom bed, and 1 st from bottom bed to top bed, using the double-ended eyelet tool.

Note that if more buttonholes are required, this sequence of one buttonhole every 18 rows may be continued for the length of the band.

COLLAR

Mattress st 4 shoulder seams before making collar.

Using ribber, cast on 85(93:103:113) sts MY and rib 30 rows T0/0. Transfer all sts to main bed.

Rt sides tog, pick up sts along neck edge main garment and replace on those already on machine. K 1 row T9 and cast off loosely.

POCKETS

RC 000 using closed-edge method, cast on 40 sts MC K T8 to row 22. Carr at Rt, bring 20 sts at opposite side of work to carr to HP. Shape

remaining 20 sts dec 1 st at both ends row every 2 rows × 3. Cast off. Repeat this shaping for 20 sts still on machine. When complete, stitch one end pocket to front side seam and one end to back side seam. Slip st pocket edges tog.

TO MAKE UP

Back st main seam from hem to cuff on either side. Slip st button band to Lt edge of garment, cont right up to collar edge. Slip st buttonhole band to Rt edge of garment including collar edge.

Sew in ends weaving back along row of self colour. Slip st cuffs and welts. Brush lightly with a teasel brush if fluffy finish is required.

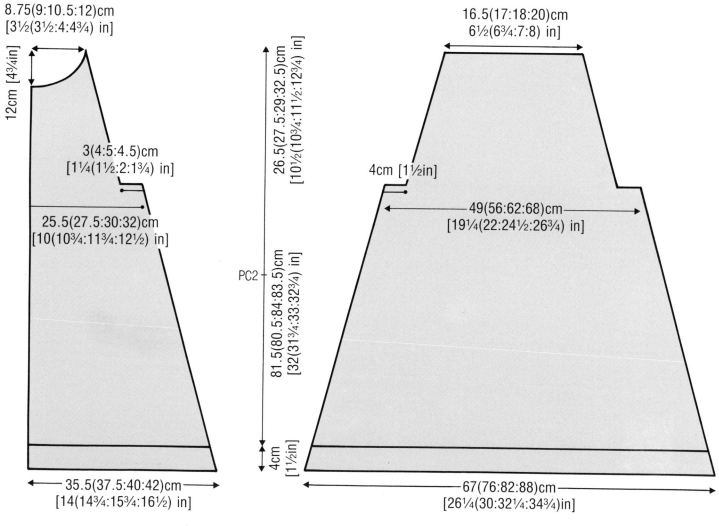

8.75(9:10.5:12)cm
[3½(3½:4:4¾) in]

12cm [4¾in]

3(4:5:4.5)cm
[1¼(1½:2:1¾) in]

25.5(27.5:30:32)cm
[10(10¾:11¾:12½) in]

35.5(37.5:40:42)cm
[14(14¾:15¾:16½) in]

26.5(27.5:29:32.5)cm
[10½(10¾:11½:12¾) in]

PC2

81.5(80.5:84:83.5)cm
[32(31¾:33:32¾) in]

4cm
[1½in]

16.5(17:18:20)cm
6½(6¾:7:8) in]

4cm [1½in]

49(56:62:68)cm
[19¼(22:24½:26¾) in]

67(76:82:88)cm
[26¼(30:32¼:34¾)in]

101

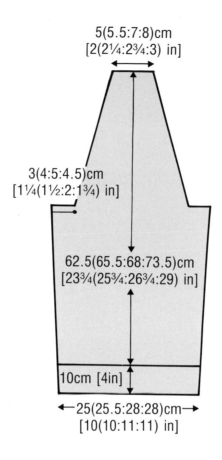

5(5.5:7:8)cm
[2(2¼:2¾:3) in]

3(4:5:4.5)cm
[1¼(1½:2:1¾) in]

62.5(65.5:68:73.5)cm
[23¾(25¾:26¾:29) in]

10cm [4in]

←25(25.5:28:28)cm→
[10(10:11:11) in]

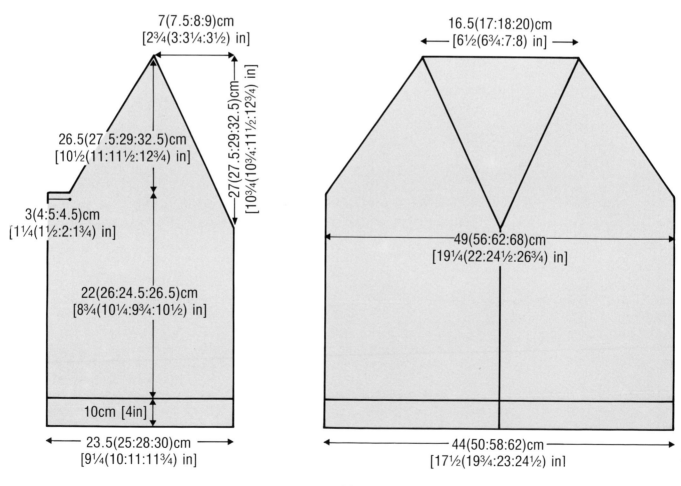

7(7.5:8:9)cm
[2¾(3:3¼:3½) in]

26.5(27.5:29:32.5)cm
[10½(11:11½:12¾) in]

27(27.5:29:32.5)cm
[10¾(10¾:11½:12¾) in]

3(4:5:4.5)cm
[1¼(1½:2:1¾) in]

22(26:24.5:26.5)cm
[8¾(10¼:9¾:10½) in]

10cm [4in]

←23.5(25:28:30)cm→
[9¼(10:11:11¾) in]

16.5(17:18:20)cm
←[6½(6¾:7:8) in]→

49(56:62:68)cm
[19¼(22:24½:26¾) in]

←44(50:58:62)cm
[17½(19¾:23:24½) in]

RAGLAN-SLEEVED CARDIGAN

TO FIT

Small: 81–87cm (32–34in)

across chest 51cm (20in)
finished length 58.5cm (23in)
sleeve length, underarm 46cm
(18in)

Medium: 91–97cm (36–38in)

across chest 54cm (21¼in)
finished length 64cm (25¼in)
sleeve length, underarm 48cm
(19in)

Large: 102–107cm (40–42in)

across chest 61cm (24in)
finished length 65cm (25½in)
sleeve length, underarm 48cm
(19in)

Extra-large: 112–122cm (44–46in)

across chest 66cm (26in)
finished length 69cm (27in)
sleeve length, underarm 51cm
(20in)

YARN

400g Gold Award mohair,
Kaleidoscope Collection, colour
number 2121 (light mauve)
A. C. Wood (speciality fibres)
Ltd, Mohair Mills, Gibson Street,
Bradford BD3 9TS

Buttons: 5

TENSION

T8
14 sts/18 rows = 10cm (4in)

Please read pattern through
carefully before starting to knit.

BACK

Cast on 62(70:80:86) sts for 1:1 rib
using the ribber. Rib 26 rows T0/0.
Transfer all sts to main bed. RC 000
T8 K to row 40(48:44:48) and at the
same time inc 1 st at either end of
row, every 4 rows until
68(78:88:96) sts. Carr at Rt. RC 000
cast off 4(6:7:6) sts at Rt edge of
work. K 1 row to Lt. Cast off
4(6:7:6) sts at Lt edge of work.
Then dec 1 st at either end of row,
fully fashioned, (using treble eyelet
tool) as follows : small : every 3
rows 6 times, every 2 rows 13
times, then K 2 rows. RC 48;
medium : every 3 rows 4 times,
every 2 rows 17 times, K 2 rows. RC
50, 24 sts remain; large : every 2
rows 24 times, K 3 rows. RC 52, 26
sts remain; extra-large : every 2
rows 28 times. RC 58, 28 sts remain.
Remove remaining sts from
machine on 6 rows WY.

FRONT

Rt front: Cast on 33(35:39:41) sts
for 1:1 rib using ribber. Rib 26 rows
T0/0. Transfer all sts to main bed.
RC 000 K straight to row
40(47:44:48) T8 and at the same
time inc 1 st at Rt edge of work
every 4 rows to 36(39:43:46) sts.
Carr at Rt.

RC 000 cast off 4(6:7:6) sts at Rt
edge of work. K 1 row to Lt. Cast
off 4(6:7:6) sts at Lt edge of work.
K 1 row. Then dec 1 st at Rt edge

of work, fully fashioned (using
treble eyelet tool), as follows .
small : at Rt edge dec 1 st every 2
rows 22 times. K 4 rows. RC 48. At
Lt edge dec 1 st every 5 rows;
medium : at Rt edge dec 1 st every
2 rows 22 times. K 4 rows. At Lt
edge dec 1 st every 5 rows. RC 50;
large : at Rt edge dec 1 st every 2
rows 25 times. At Lt edge dec 1 st
every 4 rows. RC 52; extra-large : at
Rt edge dec 1 st every 2 rows 27
times. At Lt edge dec 1 st every 5
rows 11 times. RC 58.

Lt front: Reverse shaping
instructions, reading Rt for Lt and
vice versa.

SLEEVE

K 2 alike. Cast on 34(36:40:40) sts
for 1:1 rib using ribber. Rib 26 rows
T0/0. Transfer all sts to main bed.
RC 000 K T8 to row 65(68:68:74)
and at the same time, inc 1 st either
end of row, as follows : small : every
5 rows 12 times, K 5 rows; medium :
every 5 rows 13 times, K 3 rows;
large : every 5 rows 13 times, every
2 rows once, K 1 row; extra-large :
every 4 rows 36 times, K 2 rows.

Carr at Rt. Cast off 4(6:7:6) sts at
Rt edge of work. K 1 row. Cast off
4(6:7:6) sts at Lt edge of work.
Then dec as follows : small : 1 st
either end of row every 3 rows 4
times, then 1 st either end of row
every 2 rows 17 times. RC 48, 7 sts
remain; medium : 1 st either end of
row every 3 rows 4 times, then 1 st
either end of row every 2 rows 17
times, K 2 rows. RC 50, 8 sts
remain; large : 1 st either end of

row every 3 rows 10 times, then 1 st either end of row every 2 rows 12 times. RC 52, 10 sts remain; extra-large : 1 st either end of row every 2 rows 26 times, K 2 rows. RC 58, 10 sts remain. Remove sts that remain on machine on 6 rows of WY.

TO FINISH

Mattress st 4 shoulder seams.

FRONT BAND

Cast on 11 sts for 1:1 rib using the ribber. Rib 346(364:374:412) rows T0/0. Make buttonholes at row 4:22:40:58:76 (5 all together) by transferring 1 st from top bed to bottom bed, and 1 st from bottom bed to top bed, using the double-ended eyelet tool.

Back st main seam from cuff to waist. Slip st cuffs and welts.

Slip st button band to front edge of cardigan. St on 5 buttons.

LACY SWEATER IN MIXED YARNS

TO FIT

Small: 81–87cm (32–34in)
across chest 53cm (21in)
finished length 56cm (22in)
sleeve length 43cm (17in)

Medium: 92–97cm (36–38in)
across chest 58.5cm (23in)
finished length 58.5cm (23in)
sleeve length 46cm (18in)

Large: 102–107cm (40–42in)
across chest 64cm (25in)
finished length 64cm (25in)
sleeve length 48.5cm (19in)

Extra-large: 112–122cm (44–48in)
across chest 66cm (26in)
finished length 69cm (27in)
sleeve length 51cm (20in)

YARN

MY – 400g Gold Award Mohair:
  a) Kaleidoscope mohair 2378 (red)
  b) Kaleidoscope mohair 2917 (green)
  c) Cocktail range mohair 3407 (dark blue)
  d) Kaleidoscope mohair 2120 (black)
CY1 and CY2 – 50g each
  a) Kaleidoscope mohair 2737 (shocking pink)
  Kaleidoscope mohair 2776 (maroon)
  b) Cocktail range mohair 3407 (dark blue)
  Kaleidoscope mohair 2225 (jade)
  c) Cocktail range mohair 3408 (purple)
  Kaleidoscope mohair 2223 (bright blue)
  d) Cocktail range mohair 3408 (purple)
  Kaleidoscope mohair 2913 (grey)
A. C. Wood (speciality fibres) Ltd, Mohair Mills, Gibson Street, Bradford BD3 9TS
CY3 –1(1:2:2) hanks each Colinette One-Zero 100% wool:
  a) Ruby 52
  b) Nauticus 57
  c) 54
  d) Charcoal 25
Colinette Yarns, Park Lane House, High Street, Welshpool, Powys, Wales.

TENSION

T8 for both stocking st and Fair Isle 14.5 sts/18 rows = 10cm (4in)

Note: This pattern relies mainly on hand-tooling, together with an 8-row Fair Isle pattern, and so could easily be achieved on one of the more basic machines such as the Bond. A little practice at hand selection of needles for Fair Isle is all that is necessary.

Please read pattern through carefully before starting to knit.

BACK

Cast on 70(86:94:97) sts in MY for 1:1 rib. T0/0 rib 20(26:26:26) rows. Transfer all sts to main bed.
Note: The use of the close-knit bar will improve the quality of the rib when knitting mohair, and make knitting easier.
　RC 000 MY T8 K 4 rows.
　* Make 1st row of holes for lace (see Chart)
Knit 2 rows CY1, make 2nd row of holes
Knit 2 rows CY3, make 3rd row of holes
Knit 2 rows CY3, make 4th row of holes
Knit 4 rows MY, make 1st row of holes
Knit 2 rows MY, make 2nd row of holes
Knit 2 rows MY, make 3rd row of holes
Knit 2 rows MY, make 4th row of holes
Knit 1 row MY. Set punchcard for Fair Isle.

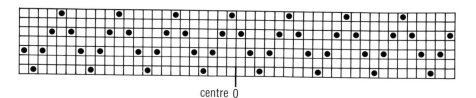

centre 0

☐ : needle in work
▣ : lace

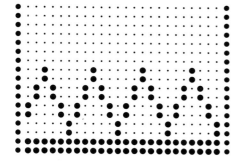

K 1 row MY start punchcard
MY feeder 1 CY2 feeder 2 K 6 rows
CY1 feeder 1 CY2 feeder 2 K2 rows
K 2 rows CY3
K 6 rows MY *

Set carr to read punchcard (see page 00). K 1 row MY. Start punchcard. Thread CY2 in feeder 2. K 6 rows. Break MY, thread CY1 in feeder 1. CY2 remains in feeder 2. K 2 rows. Remove punchcard. K 2 rows Colinette. K 6 rows MY. * Pattern repeats from * to *.

K in pattern to row 82(88:98:106). Shape back neck,

cont in pattern, as follows : set carr for Hold. All Ns to Lt of centre in HP and 12(12:14:15) to Rt. *Note* : If your machine does not have a HP, take the appropriate number of sts back to NWP using a piece of nylon cord (see page 00).

K 1 row Rt to Lt. Bring 1 N to HP. K 1 row to Rt. Bring 1 N to HP, etc until 15(15:17:18) Ns to Rt of centre are in HP. Finish at row 86(92:102:110). Break yarn. Thread up WY, K 6 rows and remove from machine. Repeat this shaping for Lt shoulder, reading Rt for Lt and vice versa.

Centre neck sts remain on machine. K 1 row in MY across these Ns T8.

Transfer alternate sts to adjacent Ns for mock 1:1 rib. K 10 rows T0, K 1 row T10. K 9 rows T0 and last row T8. Break off MY leaving a long end to sew up with. Thread up WY. K 6 rows and remove from machine.

FRONT

As for back to row 66(72:82:90). Shape neck as follows : all Ns to Lt centre in HP and 4 to Rt. Set carr for Hold. K 1 row to Lt. Bring 1 N forward to HP. K 1 row to Rt. Bring 1 N forward, etc until 15(15:17:18) Ns to Rt centre are in HP. K in pattern to row 86(92:102:110). Break yarn. Thread up WY and K 6 rows. Remove from machine.

Repeat this shaping for Lt shoulder, reversing instructions.

Centre neck sts remain on machine. Pick up sts along remainder of neck edge, leaving every 4th one. K 1 row across these Ns in MY T8. Transfer alternate sts to adjacent Ns for mock rib. K 10 rows T0. K 1 row T10. K 9 rows T0 and last row T8. Break MY. Thread up WY. K 6 rows and remove from machine.

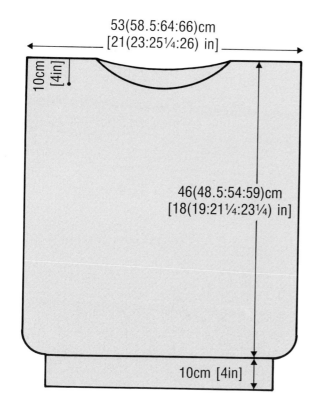

53(58.5:64:66)cm
[21(23:25¼:26) in]
10cm [4in]
46(48.5:54:59)cm
[18(19:21¼:23¼) in]
10cm [4in]

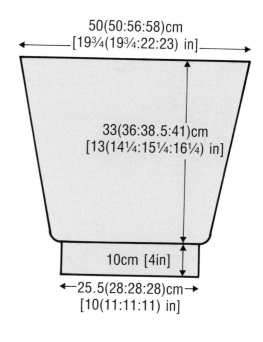

50(50:56:58)cm
[19¾(19¾:22:23) in]
33(36:38.5:41)cm
[13(14¼:15¼:16¼) in]
10cm [4in]
25.5(28:28:28)cm
[10(11:11:11) in]

SHOULDER SEAM

With front of garment facing you,
replace sts of left shoulder on
machine. Take back of garment,
and with Rt sides tog, replace sts of
Lt shoulder on Ns already in use.
Pull out WY. K 1 row MY T8 and
cast off loosely, going in front of
sinker gates. Use a claw weight and
hang from just beneath st being
cast off. This helps to stretch the st
and prevent knitting becoming too
tight.

SLEEVE

Cast on 36(40:40:40) sts in MY for
1:1 rib. Rib 20(20:26:26) rows T0/0.
Transfer all sts to main bed.
    RC 000 K in pattern as before,
except that on the second band of
the pattern in small and medium
sizes, only 2 rows of Colinette wool
are used where normally there
would be 4. The second 2 rows are
knitted in MY. K to row
60(66:70:74), *at the same time* inc
1 st at the carr side every other row
to 60(60:66:74) sts, then every 4th
row to 80(80:88:94) sts. At row
60(66:70:74) cast off very loosely as
before.

TO MAKE UP

Back st sleeve head to shoulder
edge of garment making sure
underarms match and centre of
sleeve head is at shoulder seam.
This will need pinning first. Pin
main seam from wrist to waist and
back st firmly. Slip st cuffs and
welts. Slip st neckband edge to
start of neckband matching st for
st. Sew in ends of pattern colours,
etc.
    Note: Pins are more effective if
put in at Rt angles to seam.

TECHNIQUES AND KNOW-HOW

CASTING ON

Closed-edge ('E-wrap') method

This is a very old-fashioned method of cast on that derives from the very early knitting machines. It is only necessary to use it when you are not making a hem or rib at the edge of the work, but do want a finished edge, eg a scarf, which will have a fringe put on later, or a baby garment which is going to have a crochet border. It is rather time consuming compared with the automatic cast on.

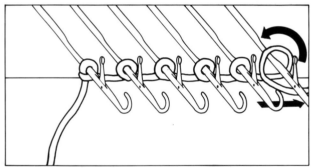

Casting on: 'E-wrap' method

Carriage at Rt.

Bring forward to WP required number of Ns. Using MY, make a simple slip knot and tie round first N at Lt. Bringing forward to HP 1 N at a time, wrap yarn round each one, as loosely as possible.

Carriage set for MT, K 1 row to Lt. Bring all Ns forward to HP, a few at a time. K 1 row to Rt. Bring all Ns forward to HP, etc and repeat. When 4 rows are complete and it is possible to hang weights, hang one claw weight in each corner and continue to knit.

Using waste yarn : nylon cord method

Carr at Rt. Using straight edge of ruler bring forward to WP required number of Ns to Lt and Rt centre 0. The best way to make sure these Ns are in the correct position and in a straight line is to take the carr across them once or twice without any yarn in. End with carr on Rt. Set st size.

Note: The st size is often referred to as tension. The round dial in the centre of the carr controls this, with numbers 1–10. The lower the number, the smaller the st; the higher the number the larger the st. A small st means tight knitting; a large st means loose knitting.

Thread up WY in feeder 1. Shut gate. Hold end of yarn firmly in Rt hand and take carr across Ns from Rt to Lt using Lt hand. A row of loops has been formed.

Take nylon cord and lay across these loops, between the N hooks and the sinker gates. The cord is not over the Ns themselves. Hold both ends of the cord below the needle bed and pull down hard. Now bring the carr across the Ns again and continue to do so, holding the nylon cord firmly all the time until 8 rows have been knitted.

Pull out the nylon cord. Break off WY. Thread nylon cord into feeder 1 just as if it were wool,

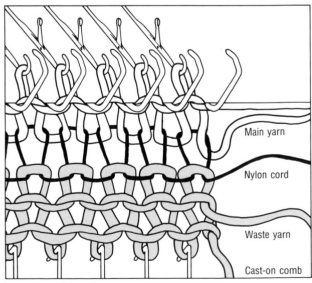

Casting on: using waste yarn

leaving about 15cm (6in) dangling below the plate. Take the longer end around behind the screw nut and under the weaving hook if there is one. Holding this long end fairly loosely in your Rt hand, take carr across to Lt of work using Lt hand. A row of sts has been formed in nylon cord. Remove nylon cord from feeder 1. Thread up MY in feeder 1. MT, K.

Using a cast-on comb : Brother machines

Bring forward to WP required number of Ns to Lt and Rt centre 0. Carr set for normal knitting (N). Thread up WY in feeder 1. Hold end of yarn in Rt hand slightly back under the machine. St size 5 or less depending on type of yarn. Take carr across once, from Rt to Lt. A row of loops has been formed. Hang the comb onto these loops and place claw weights along the length of the comb at even intervals. K 6 rows WY before breaking off and knitting 1 row of nylon cord, etc and continue as for method above.

Automatic method

Carr at Rt. Bring forward to WP required number of Ns to Lt and Rt centre 0. Using ruler provided

bring every other one of these Ns forward to HP. Set carr with side levers forward, weaving brushes down and st size 5 or lower (Knitmaster). (Jones/Brother machines are similar except that there are no side levers). Make sure the machine is set for normal knitting. Thread up yarn in feeder 1. Draw end of yarn out from under sinker plate and lay across Ns in HP behind the latches, from Rt to Lt. Holding the end of the yarn in your Lt hand take carr across Ns from Rt to Lt slowly. Continue knitting, returning weaving brushes to 'up' position after 4 rows. (Knitmaster machines side levers back after 4 rows.)

NEEDLE POSITIONS

NWP: the Ns are back in rest, they cannot knit.
WP: the Ns will always knit whatever the setting of the carr.
HP: the carr is set for Hold, these Ns will not knit.
LWP: the carr is set for normal knitting, these Ns will knit.

Try these positions out without any yarn in the machine. Take the carr across and back a few times for each position.

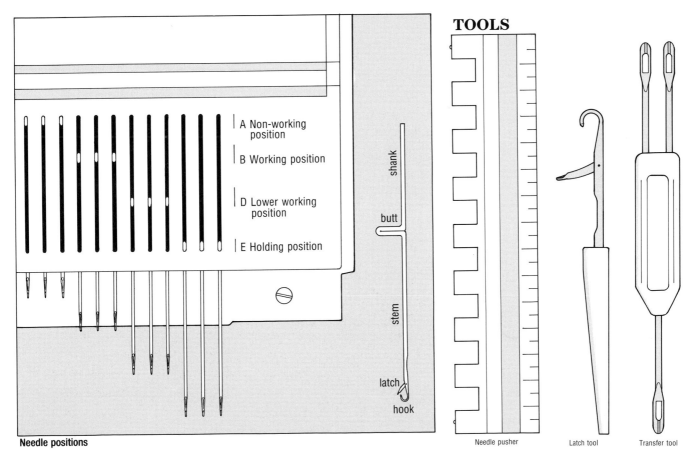

A Non-working position

B Working position

D Lower working position

E Holding position

shank

butt

stem

latch

hook

TOOLS

Needle pusher

Latch tool

Transfer tool

Needle positions

CASTING ON FOR A MOCK RIB

1:1
Carr at Rt. Using 1:1 edge of ruler bring forward to WP every alternate N up to required number of Ns. Make sure the remaining Ns really are back in NWP. Thread up WY in feeder 1 as before and shut gate. Hold end of yarn below carr firmly in Rt hand. Set st size. Take carr across from Rt to Lt with Lt hand. A row of loops is formed. Hang nylon cord over loops between N hooks and sinker gates. Pull down hard by holding both ends of nylon cord beneath the machine. Take carriage across again and continue knitting to 6 rows. Hang claw weights at either edge of work. Pull out nylon cord. Break off WY. Thread nylon cord in feeder 1 around screw nut and hold in Rt hand. K 1 row from Rt to Lt. Take nylon cord out of feeder 1. Thread up MY in feeder 1. MT K 1 row. T0 K 10 rows. T10 K 1 row. T0 K 10 rows. MT K 1 row. Using single transfer tool pick up large loops from first rows sts in MY, placing them on Ns that are empty and bringing these Ns right out to HP as you do so. At the same time hold knitting back against machine with other hand. When this is complete there should be 1 st on every N. Set tension dial to MT and take carr across. Make sure

that it is set for normal knitting. Pull out nylon cord. Continue knitting.

2:1
Arrange Ns in WP following diagram.

Follow the method for 1:1 rib above until you are ready to pick up the sts from the 1st row in MY. Using single transfer tool pick up 2nd st of the pair and the big st in between each pair. This big st goes onto the N that has no st on it. You do not need to pick up the Lt hand st of each pair. Bring the Ns right out to HP as you do this and hold the knitting back against the machine with your other hand.

Continue as for mock 1:1 rib above.

Finishing mock ribs
Once the garment piece is complete and off the machine insert a long ruler or a knitting needle into the hem and holding the main garment piece firmly in one hand pull the hem downwards. The knitting can also be steamed like this to set the sts. It is not advisable to put the iron down on the knitted fabric when doing this. If you have a steam iron hold it above the knitting and press the jet of steam button, so that only the steam touches the work. Gently pat into shape.

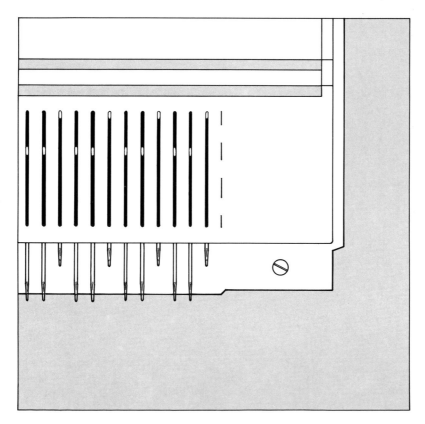

Casting on for 2:1 mock rib: needle positions

CASTING OFF

Behind sinker gates

Finish knitting with carr at either Rt or Lt depending on which end of the work you feel most comfortable working from. Using the single eyelet transfer tool, draw the first N with a st on it right out towards you, as far as it will go. Keeping your tool level with this N, push it back so that the st on the N slips off onto your tool. Still keeping the tool level, lift it up and behind the sinker gate until you can catch the end of the next N with the eyelet. Pull this N right out towards you, at the same time holding the knitting firmly back against the machine with your other hand.

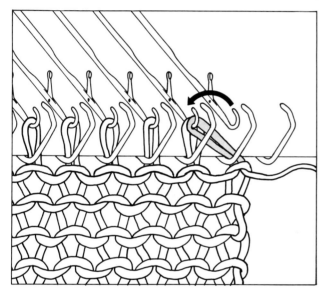

Casting off behind sinker gates

Take the eyelet tool off N and place loose end of yarn across this N behind hook and in front of latch. Pull N back into WP with your thumb and repeat. You are making a chain as in crochet.

The sts are all held in tension by the sinker gates and you will find that the cast-off row does not pull up tight or gather. Consequently you will have shoulder seams, etc that lie flat.

With claw weight

If for some reason casting off behind the sinker gates is not appropriate, eg the sleeve edge of a batwing, you can still use this method, but take the stitch in front of the sinker gate, so long as you keep at least one claw weight hanging immediately below where you are casting off. This will keep the fabric stretched and prevent it pulling up too tight. When hanging the claw weight, hang it by just one claw, at the edge. Practice will tell how far to allow the st to stretch before continuing on to the next one. The art is to achieve an even cast off which is loose enough to match the tension of the knitted stitch in the main garment. Obviously the claw weight needs to be moved frequently.

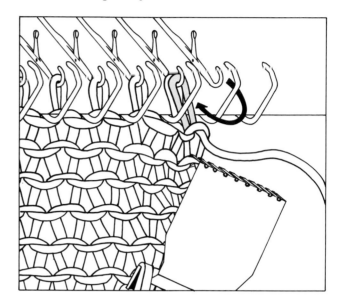

Casting off with claw weight

Picking up a stitch and casting off at the same time

This method of cast off is applicable where the two pieces of knitting to be joined may not be stretched out evenly along the bed of the machine, as in the case of a ribbed collar which is to be joined to a round neck. Both shoulder seams must be complete as the collar opening is at the centre front, so the neck edge cannot be stretched out to match the collar itself. If the collar has been knitted on the ribber, all the stitches are already transferred to the single bed.

Starting at the centre front garment, pick up 1st st and replace it on 1st st at Lt/Rt end of collar, with Rt side garment facing collar. Bring this N forward to HP using a single eyelet transfer tool. Using MY put yarn across N in front of latch. Take N back to NWP, stretching new st sufficiently to achieve a loose cast off. Place claw weight immediately below st being cast off and keep moving it as work progresses. Transfer this new st to adjacent N and repeat.

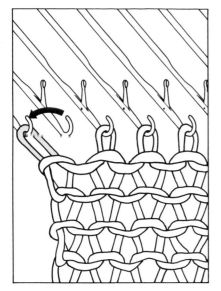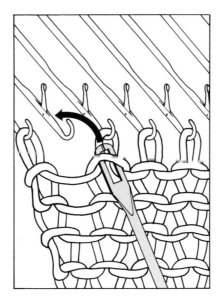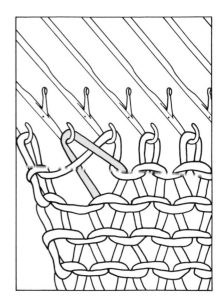

Fully fashioned increase

INCREASING

Increasing in stocking stitch
Increasing when knitting stocking stitch is unbelievably easy. All that is necessary is to bring one N forward to WP at either edge of the work, every other row. This basic method can be varied. For instance, if the machine will only form a new st at the right-hand edge when the carriage is at the Rt, do not bring forward the left-hand N until the carriage is at the Lt.

Most machines will not accept the first method whilst knitting Fair Isle. Some will accept the second method for Fair Isle. It does not however produce a very neat edge, nor does it have a fully fashioned finish.

Fully fashioned increase
Take the double eyelet tool and move the 2 end Ns out one space so that there are 2 Ns in work at edge of knitting and then 3rd one in from edge is empty. Using the single eyelet tool, pick up st below 2nd st in from edge and place it on N out of work. Repeat this process at opposite edge.

This method is particularly suitable for Fair Isle, tuck or slip stitch. It can be used to great effect, on stocking stitch. A more pronounced effect will be obtained by using the triple eyelet tool.

DECREASING

Single eyelet transfer tool
The simplest decrease is achieved by using the single eyelet transfer tool, taking end st and placing this on top of next st in, eg place transfer tool over hook of outside edge N. Keep tool level and bring N right out towards you. Push N back so that st slips off N onto tool. Still keeping tool level, lift it sufficiently to catch hold of next N in and let st slide off tool onto N, by tipping tool up slightly. Repeat this process at opposite end of row and continue knitting.

This method is the equivalent of 'knit two sts together' in hand knitting.

With certain yarns, especially synthetics, this method can give a very tight edge to the work. It can then be extremely difficult to pick up edge sts later on for a neckband, or seam, etc.

Double or treble eyelet transfer tool
A more sophisticated finish as well as a looser edge is obtained by using the double or treble eyelet transfer tool. Follow the illustrations step by step:

1) Using the double eyelet tool and keeping it level with the needles, bring forward the 2 Ns at edge of work.
2) Push back into WP so that sts slip off 2 Ns onto tool.
3) Keeping tool level lift slightly.
4) Place sts on 2nd and 3rd Ns in from edge.
5) Tip tool slightly so that sts slip off.
6) There are now 2 sts on 2nd N in from edge.
   Repeat this at opposite edge of work. The method is the same for the treble eyelet tool

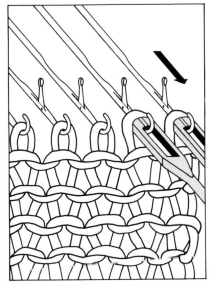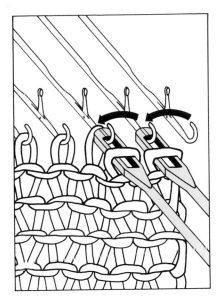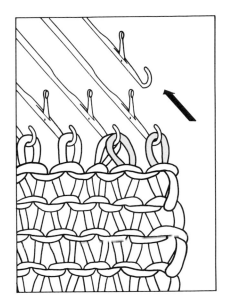

Decreasing using double or treble eyelet transfer tool

except that in this case the 3rd N in has 2 sts on it. Follow illustrations for method. Both methods give a fully fashioned finish on the right side of the work.

USE OF THE HOLDING POSITION

Shaping

Shaping using the holding position is often referred to as 'partial knitting'. Shoulder graduations are a very good example of the use of this position. This method may be used when following a written pattern where casting off is recommended for the shoulder, or when following the Knitradar/Knitleader chart. If you are using a charting device, turn the chart up by hand, from the point at which the shoulder shaping starts. Make a note of the number of rows from this point to the very last stitch. Divide this number by two. (You will be decreasing every other row.) Now divide the total number of stitches in the shoulder by the number which resulted from the first division. This will give you the number of stitches to be decreased each time.

Example Turn the chart up by hand to last point on shoulder : 20 rows. Divide this by 2 : 20 ÷ 2 = 10. Total number of stitches in shoulder = 50.

50 ÷ 10 = 5. Number of stitches to be decreased each time = 5.

Right shoulder (wrong side facing): Set carriage for hold. Knit 1 row from Rt to Lt. Bring 4

Ns at Rt edge to HP. K 1 row to Rt. Bring 1 more N forward to HP. K 1 row to Lt. Bring 4 Ns forward to HP at Rt edge, etc until all the Ns are in HP and carr is at Lt. Set carr for normal knitting and K 1 row. Break off MY, thread up WY. K 6 rows and remove from machine.

Second shoulder: Reverse shapings so that needles in HP start from Lt edge and work inwards.

Round neck shaping

Carr at Rt. Set for Hold. Bring forward to HP all Ns to Lt centre 0 and 4 to Rt centre 0. K 1 row to Lt. Bring forward to HP 1 N. K 1 row to Rt. Bring forward to HP 1 N, etc until required number of Ns are in HP. K to final row. Remove shoulder from machine on 6 rows WY. With carr still set for hold, take across to Lt side of work.

Push all except 4 Ns to Lt centre 0 back to LWP. Thread MY and K 1 row to Rt. Bring 1 N forward to HP. K 1 row to Lt.

Bring 1 N forward to HP, etc until required number of Ns are in HP. K to final row, then remove shoulder from machine on 6 rows WY. Centre neck sts remain on machine. Set carr to normal knitting and K 6 rows WY before removing from machine.

USE OF NYLON CORD

This can be used where holding position is either unsuitable or not possible on particular make of machine. On a very basic machine, there may not

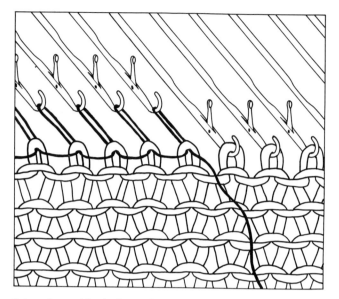

Using nylon cord for shaping

be a holding position. In this case the nylon cord can be used to remove needles from work without actually losing the stitches. It is also useful when knitting in a very light colour which could be marked by the movement of the carriage across the work while shaping.

Take a long end of nylon cord and loop over first st at Lt edge of work. Take N right back to NWP then loop nylon cord over next N and repeat. Make sure that Ns do not creep forward as you do this. If they are not all firmly back in NWP they will tend to knit. All Ns that would normally be in HP should be on nylon cord. Then K 1 row to Lt and K 1 N back on nylon cord. K 1 row to Rt, etc. When neck and shoulder shapings are complete, and both shoulders removed from machine on WY, bring nylon cord up and replace sts one by one on Ns. Remove nylon cord and continue as usual.

USE OF KNITTING-IN ELASTIC

Many yarns, particularly chunky ones, can lack elasticity. Cotton is a prime example. This can sometimes result in a floppy rib, that quickly loses its shape. To counteract this, knitting-in elastic is combined with the main yarn for the first few rows. It is not necessary to keep it in for the whole rib, although some people prefer to do this. This is obtainable from any good suppliers or by mail order from BSK Ltd, Unit 8, Murdock Road, Manton Industrial Estate, Bedford, UK (Tel: 0234 217096).

SHOULDER SEAM

Left front With Rt side work facing, take front of garment and replace Lt shoulder sts on machine. Unravel WY.*

Place back of garment against front with Rt sides facing.

Pick up sts along Lt shoulder edge, placing them on same Ns as those of the front. Unravel WY and pull out. K 1 row MT then cast off behind sinker gates.

For a shoulder seam with a garter st finish, at * K 1 row MT before putting sts from back shoulder onto machine.

HOW TO TAKE EXTRA PATTERN COLOURS UP THE SIDE OF WORK WITHOUT BREAKING YARN

When knitting Fair Isle, as each pattern colour is finished with, instead of breaking yarn, remove from feeder and tuck securely under end of top bed machine. K 2 rows then K pattern colour into end st before continuing. This can be done with any number of colours and makes a much more even edge to work than if all ends are cut. It also saves a great deal of sewing up.

This technique can be applied to ends that have been cut. If these are knitted in every couple of rows for a short distance, there will be very little sewing up later on.

It is a very secure finish.

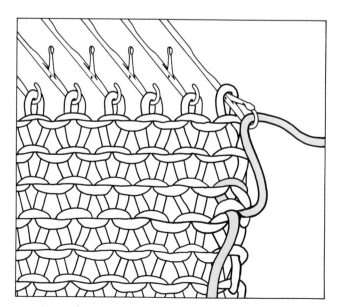

Taking pattern colours up edge of work

CABLES (Examples on pages 118–19)

Cable over 4 needles Cross sts 1 and 2 over 3 and 4 in every group of 4, right across the bed. K 6 rows. Repeat. Before knitting row 6 each time, bring empty Ns to WP. This creates extra yarn with which to make the cable. Return to NWP before cabling. K.

The ladder formed by the empty N, in each case, is latched up using the latch tool on the back of the work when the last row is reached.

Cable over 6 needles Cross sts 3 and 4 over sts 1 and 2. K 2 rows. Cross sts 3 and 4 over sts 5 and 6. K 2 rows. These 4 rows form pattern. Before knitting 2nd row each time, bring Ns from NWP to WP and K. Return empty Ns to NWP. This creates extra yarn for twisting cable.

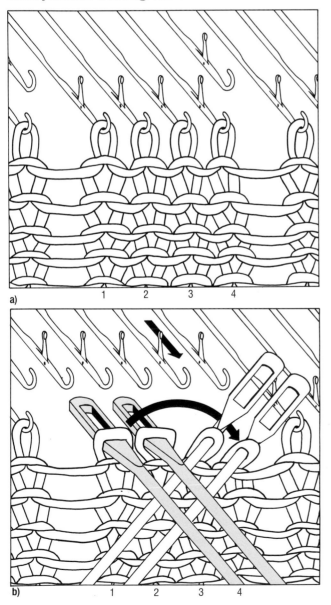

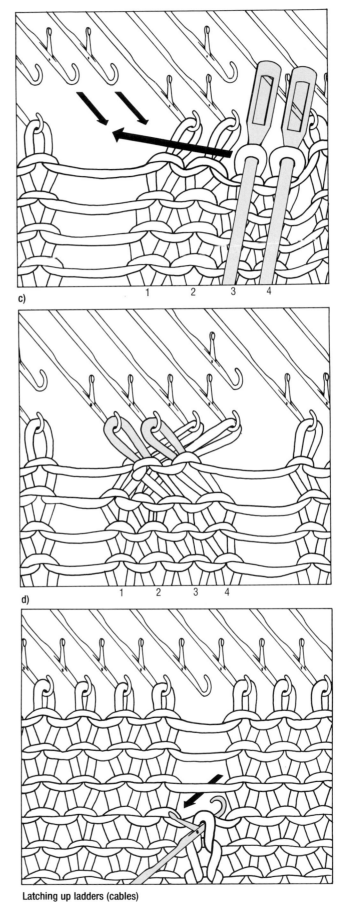

Latching up ladders (cables)

BUTTONHOLES

Buttonholes in a 1:1 ribbed band

This is knitted from top to bottom : using ribber, cast on 11 sts for 1:1 rib. T0/0 K 4 rows. Using double-ended transfer tool, take 1 st at centre knitting bottom bed, and transfer it diagonally to N top bed. Then transfer adjacent st top bed diagonally to N bottom bed. K 10 rows and repeat.

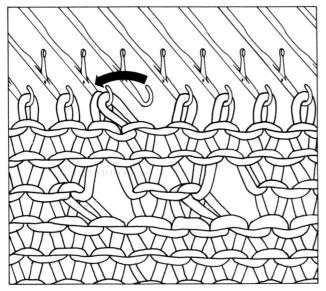

Buttonholes in a 1:1 ribbed band

Buttonholes in a 2:1 ribbed band

This is placed sideways onto the garment : using ribber cast on required number of sts for 2:1 rib. Rib 4 rows at recommended tension. Then using double-ended transfer tool, transfer 1 st from bottom to top bed and 1 st from top to bottom bed, next to one another, at even intervals across the work. K 1 row, then K each st back by hand. K 3 rows before transferring sts to main bed.

Buttonholes in a stocking st band

Cast on using WY over all Ns. K 6 rows. Break WY, join in MY, K 1 row MT, 3 rows T4 whole numbers tighter. Using short end WY, K 4 sts by hand at even intervals along band. K 4 rows tight tension. K 1 row T10. K 4 rows tight tension. Using single eyelet transfer tool take 1st st on WY at Lt and transfer to N immediately above. K back, then transfer this st to adjacent N and K back. Repeat these 2 processes for each st on WY (there are 5). The last st does not have to be knitted back twice, only once, leaving 4 empty Ns. Pick up the 4 loops from below the WY and place these on the 4 empty Ns. Repeat for each buttonhole.

When this stage is complete, K 4 rows tight tension before picking up 1st row of loops in MY in each case. K 1 row MT.

Attach to main garment piece as shoulder seam.

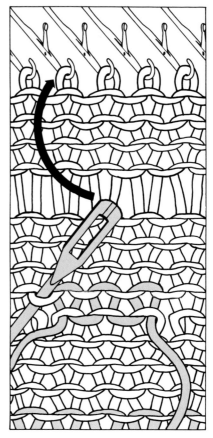

Buttonholes in a stocking st band

LACE

On the chunky machine, whatever model you have, true eyelet hole lace must be done manually. A lacy fabric can be produced on both Knitmaster and Brother machines with punchcards but this is completely different. The machine manual will tell you which punchcards are suitable for this and the way to set up your machine to achieve it.

Eyelet hole lace

Take a simple zig-zag pattern : this can be achieved by transferring a stitch to the adjacent needle every time a hole is required. Use the single eyelet transfer tool.

It is usual to start from the centre of the bed and work outwards. All sts to Lt centre are moved to Lt and all sts to Rt centre are moved to Rt.

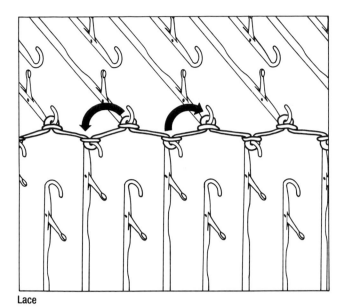

Lace

Once all the sts for a particular row have been transferred, the row is knitted. Then a second row is knitted. Sts are never transferred on adjacent rows in manual lace.

The advantage of this method is that there are no restrictions on the width or length of the pattern. Anything that can be planned out on squared paper is possible. It is extremely quick to do particularly on chunky yarn.

KNITTED CORD

Using closed-edge method, cast on over 3 sts. K 3 rows. Set carr to slip in 1 direction only. K. When cord has reached required length, cast off.

NECKBANDS

Basic single-bed method

This often proves appropriate on the chunky machine even when a true rib has been used for welts and cuffs, particularly when knitting with mohair. It tends to gather the neck in sufficiently for a good fit, and lies neatly.

When neck shaping using HP is complete, centre neck sts remain on machine. Pick up sts either side of these, every loop and every other 'knot', ie ¾ of the total number of sts. Set carr for normal knitting. Thread MY and K 1 row MY. Transfer alternate sts to adjacent Ns in preparation for mock 1:1 rib. T0 K 10 rows. T10 K 1 row. T0 K 10 rows. Break MY, thread WY, K 6 rows and remove work from machine.

Repeat this neckband for back of garment. There will be two shoulder seams, rather than one.

Neckband knitted on the ribber

This neckband is knitted in one piece with a single seam on one shoulder. One shoulder seam of garment should be completed before knitting neckband.

With ribber in place cast on 80 sts for 2:1 rib. T0/0 rib 9 rows T6/6 rib 1 row. Transfer all sts to main bed. K 1 row MT. Take main garment pieces and lay along edge neckband. Pick up ¾ neck edge sts and all sts in WY. K 1 row MT. Cast off loosely.

Cut and sew

Mark out neck shape on garment using tailor's chalk, after both shoulder seams are complete. Using zig-zag setting on sewing machine, or overlocker if you have one, st around just inside this line twice. Using sharp scissors cut along line of tailor's chalk. Take neckband and pin in place, starting from shoulder seam. It may need easing. Back st through row of loops next to WY on outside of work, and slip st through loops on inside of garment. Pull out WY. This gives a very neat and professional finish.

Cut and Sew Neckband with Ribber
With ribber in place cast on required number of sts in MY for 2:1 rib. T0/0 rib 9 rows, T6/6 rib 1 row. Bring all empty Ns into WP and set carr for full N rib. K 1 row. Set carr for tubular or circular knitting and reset tension accordingly. K 6 rows on back and 6 on front bed. Break MY, thread WY and K 6 more rows back and front. Break WY and remove neckband from machine.

Cut and sew neckband for single-bed machines
Using WY cast on required number of sts over all Ns. K 6 rows MT. Break WY, thread MY and K 6 rows at least 2 whole numbers tighter than MT. Transfer every 3rd st to adjacent N for 2:1 rib. K 8 rows on tightest possible tension. K 1 row T10, K 8 rows tight tension. Bring empty Ns into work and K 6 rows MT minus 2. Break MY, thread WY, K 6 rows MT. Break WY and remove from machine.

This can now be used in exactly the same way as the neckband knitted using the ribber.

POCKETS

In a side seam
T8 RC 000 using closed-edge method, cast on 40 sts MY. K T8. RC 22 carr at Rt, bring 20 sts at opposite side work to carr, to HP. Shape remaining 20 sts : dec 1 st at both ends rows

every 2 rows 3 times. Cast off.

Repeat this shaping for 20 sts still on machine. This pocket piece is folded in half and the two straight edges are stitched to the side seams of the main garment. The edges of the pocket are slip-stitched together, then the side seam of the garment is back-stitched as usual but of course, not across the pocket opening.

Square pocket in main garment piece
Once welt is complete, K to top of pocket opening. Carr at Rt, set for Hold. Make a note of row number. Break yarn. At Lt side of work, put all Ns to Lt of 20 in HP. At Rt side of work, put all Ns to Rt of 20 in HP. There should now be 40 Ns in work, in the centre.

Transfer every alternate st to adjacent N out of this 40, for a 1:1 rib, or every 3rd N for a 2:1 rib. Replace weights on this centre 40 sts and move them up frequently as you knit. K approximately 10 rows st size 3, 1 row st size 10, 10 rows st size 3. Change to a st size 2 whole numbers tighter than main tension, and K 50 rows, depending on required length of pocket. Carr at Rt. RC back to row noted down. Break MY. Set carr for normal knitting and continue pattern.

Make up by pinning the pocket welt in place on Rt side garment and slip st down neatly. On wrong side garment, slip st both Lt and Rt edges of pocket 'bag'.

MAKING UP

Slip stitch

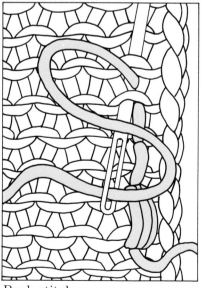

Back stitch

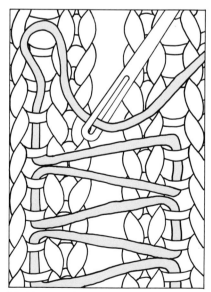

Mattress st

NOTES FOR KNITTING MOHAIR

Close-knit bar When knitting with chunky mohair, always use the close-knit bar as this makes the knitting easier and gives a better rib. Sts at the edge of the work will be less likely to drop.

Silicone spray Spray the cone of mohair with a silicone spray the night before you intend to knit with it, and seal it into a plastic bag. *Do not* spray the machine. This makes the mohair go through the machine more smoothly.

Weights Chunky mohair generally needs all the weight that is available. Keep the ribber comb and weights in place for as long as possible. When this is no longer possible, eg shaping neck, use claw weights and keep pulling the work down.

TENSION SWATCH

Using closed-edge method, cast on over 40 sts. RC 000 K 10 rows MY. Using contrast yarn of same thickness, K 2 rows. RC 000. MY K 15 rows. Using contrast yarn place markers on 11th N either side centre 0. This is done by bringing the 11th N out to HP and hanging a short length contrast yarn into the hook. The N is then taken back to WP. K 15 rows. RC 30. Remove MY, thread CY and K 2 rows. Break CY, thread MY and K 10 rows. Cast off. Pull swatch lengthwise to set sts.

The swatch must be treated in exactly the same way as the garment itself, so if the yarn is pure wool, or cotton, the swatch can be steam pressed. If the yarn is an oiled wool, the swatch must be washed according to the yarn supplier's instructions and when dry, steam pressed. In either case, it should be left to rest after pressing, before measuring. Synthetics must be treated

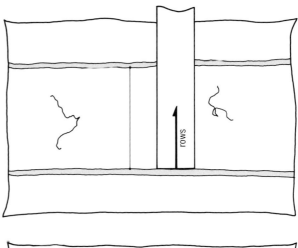

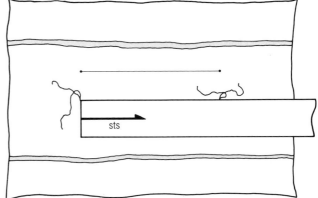

Tension swatch

differently and that is beyond the scope of this book.

When the swatch has rested sufficiently, pin out on smooth surface, eg padded ironing board. Put pins in at even intervals, 1cm (0.4in) apart, at right angles to knitting. Do not pull or stretch swatch as you do this. Make sure it is square. Take a ruler and measure between 2 markers. 20 sts = ? cm, then measure between 2 stripes CY : 30 rows = ? cm.

YARN BROKERS

All do mail order. Most have American distributors.

A. C. Wood (speciality fibres) Ltd
Mohair Mills, Gibson Street, Bradford BD3 9TS
Texere Yarns
College Mill, Barkerend Road, Bradford BD3 9AQ
Colinette Yarns
Park Lane House, High Street, Welshpool
Powys, Wales
J. Hyslop Bathgate & Co
Victoria Works, Galashiels, Scotland TD1 1NY
Designer Yarns
PO Box 18, Longcroft, Keighley BD21 5AU
T. M. Hunter Ltd
Sutherland Wool Mills, Brora, Scotland KW9 6NA
Jamieson & Smith (Shetland Wool Brokers) Ltd
90 North Road, Lerwick, Shetland Isles ZE1 0PQ

Nethy Products
Kirkshaws Road, Coatbridge, Scotland ML5 4SL
Yeoman Yarns Ltd
31 High Street, Kibworth, Leicestershire LE8 0HS

Designer Yarns distributor in USA
Peter Sagal
Silk City Fibres
155 Oxford Street, Paterson, New Jersey 07522
USA (Tel: 0101 201 942 1100)

Australia:
International PTY Ltd
Tex Yarns, 161 Abbot Street, Sandringham 3191
Victoria, Australia

ACKNOWLEDGEMENTS

A great many people have contributed their time and skills very generously to this book. Norma Gayton has knitted enthusiastically through almost all the patterns, unafraid to tell me when I was wrong, and warm in her praise of colour schemes she liked.

John Melville took the wonderful photographs.

Tony Weaver drew the diagrams and charts and helped art direct the photographs.

Helen, Angie, Nardis, June, Julia, Nuno, Gareth and Lyndon modelled the garments and had a lot of fun.

R. C. Austin of Newton Abbot were responsible for the accessories for the majority of the pictures, supplying jewellery, clothing and equipment endlessly.

The Moorland Rambler in Exeter supplied the climbing rope and clothing; Ian Gardiner the men's trousers and top. A host of willing friends lent their own gear including cricket bats, pads, etc and brought their prized motorbike and vintage car for photo sessions. Ginny Cox made me very welcome in her house. I would like to thank those whose allotment we trampled on and whose beautiful gardens we enjoyed.

I am indebted to the many wool brokers who supplied the yarn for their support and co-operation.

My grateful thanks to all of you. I hope you agree it was worth it.

INDEX

Page references in *italic* indicate illustrations